SURVIVING

SURVIVING:

BUILT FOR THE CHALLENGE

JUANITA GREGG

Columbus, Ohio

Surviving: Built for the Challenge

Published by Gatekeeper Press
2167 Stringtown Rd, Suite 109
Columbus, OH 43123-2989
www.GatekeeperPress.com

Library of Congress Control Number: 2021943222

ISBN (paperback): 9781662916069
eISBN: 9781662916076

Juanita Gregg had a sharp pain in her abdomen and is shocked to learn from her gastroenterologist that she had inherited a family trait of colorectal cancer. SURVIVING: Built for the Challenge tells her arduous journey of crises with health and family. She, at first, thought this test was only for her and couldn't understand why each time she overcame a test, another test was just around the corner. Her sisters, son and husband are her biggest cheerleaders and then the unthinkable happens. Her husband, Wesley, is diagnosed with a condition and, if he is not treated, he will not survive past one year.

In Loving Memory of

Mom and Dad, who raised me and helped show me who I wanted to be in life. Thank you for guiding me and for your unconditional love. Mom you have prayed for me and encouraged me to always put God first in everything I do.

Stanley, my brother, you encouraged me to keep it moving and not to look back at what could have been. Thank you for being that example of what higher education can help a person accomplish in life.

And

My dear husband, Wesley Gregg, Sr., thank you for supporting and helping me through each difficult period in my life. And thank you for your love, commitment, confidence and for always telling me to never give up, which helped me be the woman I am today.

I will forever love you all!

Contents

Dedication

To my parents, my brother, my husband, and extended family, and to all those strong men and women in my life who continue to help me be strong.

————

To the loves of my life:
Stephen, my most caring and handsome son,
you are precious to me and my reason for being,
and finally, to my sisters, Linda and Janice for always being there for me and encouraging me.

Acknowledgements

First, I want to thank the Lord Jesus Christ who has given me the opportunity to survive the trials and tribulations so that I may encourage others that He is the way, the truth and the life. It is only through Him that all things are possible. He is my strength and my all. I give Him all the glory and honor and I praise His holy name.

Thanks to my pastor, elders, ministers, evangelists and all my church family, for lifting me up and keeping me in your prayers. Thanks to my two best girlfriends who always check up on me in good and bad times in my life. Thank you to my family and to all my friends who always told me that I had a story to tell which led me to write a book, *SURVIVING: Built for the Challenge,* that will encourage others.

Foreword

For many years, I wondered why a book should be written about my life's struggles. After much prayer and hearing the struggles of others, it became apparent to me that being transparent and reading about other people's struggles was encouraging. I learned it is through our struggles that the spirit-man can be lifted.

Therefore, it is my hope and prayer that, while gaining insight on my personal struggles and the victories won, you, too, will be encouraged, strengthened, hopeful and even become a catalyst to encourage and inspire others. In doing so, you will be enabled to challenge others to look at their situation in a more positive manner.

When reading this book, it points you to the Word of God, and the principles and promises therein. God's promises cannot go void. This book challenges you to examine your struggles and not give up hope, but rather turn to God. Know that with God on your side, you can make it. Indeed, God performed miracles as mentioned in the Bible, and God continues to perform miracles today. Understand that through life's journey, there will be challenges but whatever is God's will, it shall be done. Be assured that God answers prayers of the righteous. He knows the desires of your heart. Though we are born of sin, it is through God's grace (which is a gift) and mercy (which is not receiving the punishment we deserve) that He gives us in our time of need. This book also encourages you to seek God in all your challenges. Seek God through continual prayers as this is the only way to have access to God's love and His assistance. There is nothing we can do without the love of God.

This book is also a reminder to keep pushing towards your goals and trust God in all you do; it serves as a reminder of the possibilities of what God can do. Be comforted in knowing that others care about you and are praying for you.

Introduction

On my way to lunch with my girlfriend, a sudden, sharp, excruciating pain hit me in my stomach. It knocked the breath out of me. I doubled over, trying to catch my breath. The only thing that helped revive me from the pain was the sudden yell of my name from my girlfriend. With tears in my eyes, I was able to catch my breath. Little did I know that my visit to my gynecologist would be the beginning of an uphill battle to survive.

All I know is that I am just an average kind of person who just wanted to have a simple, happy life, fulfilling my passion for teaching. I was determined that nothing would prevent me from attaining my desire, or so I thought.

As far as I can remember, my aspiration was to be a teacher. There were no long lists of scholars in our family that I was aware of, but helping others and showing others how to do something felt good to me. There were many times in my younger years that I would daydream about teaching, not in a specific topic, but general teaching in an elementary school. My daydreaming while watching television would be interrupted by my siblings who would be arguing over what show to watch. The interruptions did not bother me too much as I knew that when bedtime came, I could lay down on my comfortable bed and dream about becoming a teacher.

Growing up in the 1960s, and in a low-income part of a city where there was gang violence, convinced my mother that this was not a place to raise her children; there had to be a way out. Most people were struggling, especially families faced with similar challenges that my family faced. There were so many different life challenges that we faced that it seemed impossible to succeed with our endeavors. Financially, going to college can put a strain on parents, or parent as was my situation. Would I ever be able to attend college to fulfill my aspirations?

Our dad, Drue Wallace Morgan, died at the early age of thirty-six from congestive heart failure, leaving our mom, born as Jean Dolores Barbour, a widow at the age of thirty-three. Mom raised four children: Stanley (Stan), who was the eldest, Linda (Lin), the oldest of the girls, then Janice (Jan), and then, of course, me, the baby of the family. At the time of Dad's death, Stan was away at school in the country up in New York state in the tenth grade, Lin was age fourteen and in the ninth grade and Jan was age twelve and in the seventh grade. I was eleven years old and in the sixth grade. I remember praying to God to spare Daddy's life. I made promises to God that if only He would let him live, I would be the best Christian there ever was. Like most children, I believed that by closing your eyes and making a wish, whatever you wished for would somehow miraculously come true. I also believed that as a child, promises could not be broken. My father didn't make it, but I still kept my promise to God.

As a young, married, working mother, I continued to focus on furthering my education. However, my pursuit was constantly interrupted by a medical family trait of colorectal cancer and family crises and simply the need to take a break to get recharged. As I walk down this arduous life journey, my faith in God and my courage are constantly tested. However, without our faith being tested, how would we get to know God or discover our inner strengths? It is through our tests or challenges that we get to know and depend on God. It is through our most difficult challenges that we realize that life is like a test and we must prepare, study and be ready for almost anything. On the other hand, even after you think you're prepared for life, there are times when you feel you are not.

My analogy is that life throws or pitches you curve balls, fast balls, slider balls, knuckleballs and knuckle-curve balls, and the results depend on the strategy you use to catch them. In my life, there were so many different types of balls thrown my way. How do our life challenges affect us spiritually? Or better yet, how does spirituality affect us?

Think about the many different "balls" that are thrown your way. Have you ever been overwhelmed by life challenges and unexpected, stressful situations? Did you wonder how you were going to overcome them? Or did you focus on how you were going to survive through challenges? Well, read further to find out how my faith and trust in God helped bring uplifting feelings and how it led to a path of victory.

CHAPTER 1

Growing with Faith

Though you surrender your life to God, it is not a promise that things will be easy. In fact, life may become that much more challenging because Satan is mad that he did not win you over, so he will continue to try to 'bait' you or use deceitfulness to bring you over to his side.

Understand that the roads we choose to follow are never free of bumps or curves; but eventually, if you keep your eye on Jesus, the turns will lead to a smoother path. In my younger years, knowing of the miracles told in the Bible, I would often think that God should make today's miracles more known to people and maybe more people would get saved. Be careful what you ask for; God knows your thoughts!

Never in my wildest dreams would I nor anyone else have thought that my life challenges would turn out to be those 'today's' miracles. It was unbelievable to me that I would be the vessel God selected to be one of His miracles and that He would use me the way that He did.

Why not, you say? Well, considering that I grew up in a strong Christian household and was practically scared of doing any of the things that other young people enjoyed, I thought I was special in God's eyes. Being "special" to me meant He loves me so much that certain hurt and harm would not touch me, and that God would even protect me from disappointments (excluding the death of my father at the tender age of eleven) as a young teenager and young woman. Was I really "special?"

My faith in God was strong as a young woman, starting at the age of nineteen. My life was "peachy peachy" as I called it. I graduated from high school with honors and was a member of the National Honor Society. I got my first job at one of the top ten chemical companies while in high school as part of the Co-Op School Work Program. I was permanently hired there on February 9, 1976, working in the stenography department. It was a department of all females and one male stenographer. It did not take long for me to realize this was not what I wanted to do nor was I good at it. Taking dictation was not for me, and my boss knew it, too.

When the offer came for a position in a different department, I immediately accepted it. Two years later, I accepted another position in one of the business departments as an Administrative Assistant working for four principals. Basically, every two years, I was promoted to various positions until I became an employee working with multiple buyers in a different department. It was in this department where my job responsibilities and positions placed me in higher levels and, of course, an increase in salary. Though I was happy and excelling in my career and in dating, I never gave up on my passion for teaching.

In January 1980, I met my first "real" boyfriend, Wesley Gregg, Sr., while on the way to work. Wesley and I dated for a truly short time and within that same year, we got engaged — love at first sight. We knew we wanted to get married — love was definitely 'in the air.' We went out on many dates; to the movies, dinner, and bowling just to name a few. If we did not go out on a date, Wesley would come over to my house. My mom was tired of us sitting comfortably on the sofa at home, night after night, and like any mother, she was concerned that something would happen. Yes, she was concerned we would have sex and I would become pregnant before marriage! When I say we dated constantly, we were at my house at least every other day after work. Mom would call me upstairs and say, "Please tell him to go home because I want to go to bed!" We obviously were keeping her awake because every fifteen minutes she would call downstairs to me asking for water or to bring her up a Pepsi. Really, this was another one of Mom's tactics to prevent us from getting into trouble.

I married the man who stole my heart, Wesley Gregg, Sr., in 1981. We had our one and only child, a beautiful son, Stephen Michael Gregg in 1985. Everything was fantastic! The Lord was blessing me, and I had no real complaints, except that I had to have a cesarean birthing our 9 lbs. 13 oz. 21 ½ inches long baby boy. I felt that I could not deliver a baby right. Immediately after the delivery, as they wheeled me to my hospital room, I recall telling Jan that it was not worth it! I said, "Don't do it!" and "It was horrible!" Yes, I took having a cesarean in a negative way.

It was a painful recovery period to say the least. Getting up to walk felt like my entire insides were falling out. The pillow they had me use to press against my abdomen to ease the pain when walking did not help much. Somehow, I got through the pain and pressed on, anticipating when I would get back in shape.

When I went for my six-week postnatal checkup, the doctor's assistant asked me, "Are you OK now?" And she followed that question with, "I heard you took it hard." I thought, *Hmmm, did I really act up? Did I use profanity, did I use obscene words, or did I act crazy?* You must understand and know me; I am not a talker, per se, and usually keep my feelings and opinions to myself. I am somewhat of an introvert. I asked the assistant to explain, and I was told that my facial expressions said everything! After a few seconds, I said, "Having a cesarean is no walk in the park."

Well, I thought having a cesarean would be the worst thing that could happen to me. I was wrong.

In years to come, little did I know, I would come across some major challenges. While home taking care of baby Stephen, I did not really feel that motherly instinct and my family recognized it. Lin stepped up to the plate and helped me during those first three important months. I think baby Stephen felt the distance I had, or felt my reservations. I assume now that it was what doctors and experts call postpartum depression. This is described as feeling inadequate, having lack of interest in your baby, and feelings of sadness and hopelessness. There is a range of postpartum symptoms, and you can search the internet for a full description and remedies. So, yes, I did have a lack of interest in my baby and did not appreciate or feel honored being a mother. Baby Stephen seemed to just look at me as if to say, "Who are you? I want the other lady." It's so amazing how an infant can pick up on your vibes!

One day, the Lord spoke to me and made me realize that, hey, that is your baby, not Lin's, and having a baby is a blessing. It took approximately three months for me to accept the fact that I was a mother. Daddy Wesley, on the other hand, he was inebriated with joy and delight with being a father again. Yes, again, for you see, Wesley had a four-year-old son when I met him. I will save that whole experience of "the other woman" for my next book.

By the age of twenty-six, with four years of marriage, baby Stephen, working every day and going to school, my life was awesome. I studied at a university campus located in the downtown area and received my Certificate of Computer Science. I then studied at the county's community college and received the President's Honor award for multiple semesters and graduated with honors. Not settling with my associate's degree, a few years later, I decided to attend a university where I received my Bachelor of Science Degree (Cum Laude) in Business Administration in 2011. There were many interruptions before I was able to finally complete my bachelor's degree program. I completed my studies with honors while being a good wife, accelerating at my job, and being the best mommy I could be. Believe me, it was hard, but I had the determination and stamina to hang in there. Thank God for Wesley and especially my mom who watched Stephen while I went to college at night. Wesley was so supportive and knew that when either one of us succeeded, we both did; we were a team, partners, lovers, and a family. Things were perfect, until they weren't.

CHAPTER 2

Testing My Faith

Life was treating Wesley and me great. We were enjoying ourselves as parents. I received job promotions and applied for positions continuously for five years in a row. We were doing great both as parents and financially. Glory be to God.

I came from a church that strongly believed in tithe paying. I can attest that when you pay your tithes, the Lord will bless you. As I recall from being a young child, we were taught that "God loveth a cheerful giver." According to the Bible, **"Every man according as he purposeth in his heart, so let him give; not grudgingly, or of necessity: for God loveth a cheerful giver" (2 Corinthians 9:7).** Giving comes from my heart, and not because I look for something back from God. Giving makes me feel good. It is a blessing to be able to bless my church and others. Because of how God has blessed us, we can not only financially give to others in need, but also help in other ways.

Being a cheerful giver is not only about money, but about giving your time, sharing your talent, or giving something that is yours without looking for something in return or making that person feel obligated to you. It was taught to me that when you tithe (10% of income), the Lord will return it ten-fold. **"Bring ye all the tithes into the storehouse, that there may be meat in mine house, and prove me now herewith, saith the LORD of hosts, if I will not open you the windows of heaven, and pour you out a blessing, that there shall not be room enough to receive it"** (Malachi 3:10).

I love giving back and working in the church. As I grew spiritually, my involvement with church activities included joining the junior ushers and joining the junior choir, both of which lead to me being a lead usher and becoming a member of the main choir. As I matured, I became one of the directresses of the main choir. Later, in my adult years, I became the Sunshine Band leader, teaching and working with children. When people say they were born in the church, well, I am one of those people. I remained at the same church for over 40 years, and currently have been a member at a different church for 18 years.

The children in the Sunshine Band were from the ages of six to twelve. Of course, my son, Stephen, and later my nephew, Tyler, were part of the group. I taught the children songs which we sang once a month. They were taught Bible verses, performed skits, and I had an assistant that helped with arts and crafts and anywhere else she was needed.

Twice a month, on Saturdays, I would transport children who required a ride to our sessions where lunch was also provided. My sister Jan would pitch in when I could no longer fit all the kids in my car. I believe that when you are doing the work of the Lord, He will provide and make a way. "Won't He do it!"

In today's time, you would not dare squeeze that many children in one car without seatbelts. God was on my side!

The parents were elated that their children looked forward to our gatherings, and I am sure they were glad to get some free time of their own. They were appreciative that I took the time to teach them. When one of the grandparents of one of my kids found out that I was providing lunch for the children, she gave me a few dollars to help! It warmed my heart and I thanked her graciously.

I loved teaching and working with children and did not mind spending money on what was needed. After all, I was blessed and paid my tithes regularly. What an awesome God we serve! According to the Bible: **"And whatsoever ye do, do it heartily, as to the Lord, and not unto men; (24) Knowing that of the Lord ye shall receive the reward of the inheritance: for ye serve the Lord Christ" (Colossians 3:23-24).**

I did not have to report to the parents what we were working on or doing, because the children were so excited at our activities they would get to the parents before I did. We tried to keep some projects under wraps until we were ready for our big performances. Oh, the joy of it all. God was working on me and molding me, giving me direction. I knew working with children was my calling. I was totally enjoying my walk of faith with God. And, I had no idea my faith would soon be put to the test.

Though working with children fulfilled my desire to teach, my everyday job also gave me a sense of fulfillment and accomplishment. At work, I continued to receive promotions. One position I held when working with multiple buyers and managers played an intricate part in my future with the company. The staff that I worked with was very vocal and made an appeal that the department head create a career path job since everyone was at the same level. I did not take part in their discussions or requests. I believe the discussions went on for a few months. One afternoon, the department head called a staff meeting to provide the staff an update on the creation of a career path position. The staff, including myself, sat in his corner office anticipating the decision.

He announced that a new position was finally created, and the person who got the assignment. Yes, it was me! Silence fell across the room and only one person congratulated me. I was stunned and speechless, and stared dumbfounded at the department head. I said in an extremely low voice, "Thank you" to him and to the one person who congratulated me. One of my co-workers looked at me and said, "You act like you don't know what he just said to you!" Visibly upset, she immediately began to cry. Again, I was speechless as other co-workers consoled her. We all walked out of the department head's office, me still stunned, while others showed disgust and anger.

Within minutes I decided to walk to the restroom to absorb what just happened. In the corridor was a board where available jobs were posted. The position that I was just assigned was posted on the board! When I read the qualifications, which included an associate's degree, I realized the job was configured around my credentials. What a blessing, as I was not part of the team that met with the department head requesting the career path job! Most of my co-workers were upset, but I did not take it personally because I understood their frustration and anger. I did empathize with them and understood how they could feel "cheated" out of the position because they were the ones who appealed for a career path job.

"What God has for me is for me" is what I leaned on. I know most people believe in the saying "the squeaky wheel gets the oil," but not in this case. I believe that sometimes, if you just sit back and do your job and don't complain, God will make it that those in higher positions will eventually see how dedicated of a worker you are. Please do not think I felt proud or would think of myself as better than my co-workers. It was just my "season." I believed that God would see to it that they get the promotion they too deserved — but in their "season."

I stayed in my little cubby as I did not want anyone to approach me as I knew there was a little animosity towards me. I thought it best to stay out of everyone's sight as much as possible; 'out of sight, out of mind.' I thought it best to just keep working and keep my mouth shut and eventually things would smooth over, which they did. Thank God!

I had no say in the appointed promotion and felt powerless and speechless, so it was better if I did not say a word to try to soften things. Feeling this way was my clue for letting God fight this battle. You do not need to say a word for the Lord will speak on your behalf and the Lord will fight your battles. **"The Lord shall fight for you, and ye shall hold your peace" (Exodus 14:14).** And guess what, most of those co-workers eventually got promotions — in their season! Look how the Lord works! Every blessing has its season.

More blessings and promotions were on the horizon and led me to traveling to France and Germany. The department rolled out a new system and my job was a pertinent piece for the process to work. The major responsibilities were to enter data, compose the standards, and include examples of dos and don'ts. After a few months, it was decided that I needed a backup person and that person worked in France. This is how I got the chance to travel to France and Germany. I did not like flying and my wonderful mother hated the idea of me flying, but I had to do what I had to do.

The next phase of my career led to more traveling. There was a need to roll out the procurement process and I was chosen to learn it and then teach it to all users, including management. I started training sessions locally, then proceeded to travel to other business locations such as Reading, PA, Louisville, KY, Knoxville, TN, Houston, TX and Chicago, IL. I enjoyed teaching others, so conducting training sessions were right up my lane. The Lord was truly blessing me. After all, I had my wonderful family, a job I loved and I was continuing my education in the evenings. My life was 'peachy peachy.' I praised God for all He was doing in my life. When the praises go up, the blessings come down!

***

One beautiful, clear afternoon in September 1999, my girlfriend and I were going on our lunch break when suddenly I got this excruciating pain in my stomach. It knocked the breath out of me. I doubled over. I could not breathe. I was gasping for air. My complexion changed and my skin became pasty, and my eyes teared up. My girlfriend screamed out my name and that is when I caught my breath. We were both frightened and cried all the way back to work. When I got to my desk, I immediately called my gynecologist. He was able to fit me in his schedule the same day I made the call. The walk to his office seemed to take longer than usual, though his office was located just a few blocks from where I worked. He was waiting for me and immediately examined me but did not find anything out of the norm.

A month later, I had my regular gynecologist appointment. From home, I got in my car, and picked up my uncle, because I had offered to take him somewhere after my appointment. My uncle waited in the car because there was no need for him to come into the office with me. No way!

When I saw my gynecologist, he said he was still concerned about my recent visit. He performed a rectal examination. The result was immediate. Unmistakably, I had colorectal cancer! No doubts about it, he said! I had blood in my stool.

I was in shock. I could not say a word. My gynecologist told me that I would need surgery and chemotherapy. *What? Me? I am only forty years old. Really?* He recommended a colonoscopy physician and made the appointment for me. There was no doubt in my mind that this thing was serious. I got in my car and could not say a word to my uncle. I just drove up I-95 in a daze. To this day, I do not know how I got him to where he needed to go and then got us both back home safely.

Once I dropped my uncle home, I drove to my mom's. I still could not cry. I told Mom the horrible result. We hugged each other and I said, "Mom, this is my personal test." Remember I mentioned that my life was 'peachy peachy,' but now I will have a true testimony. I thought if God did not say so then this cannot be true. My mind raced to the scripture that states if man gives a report that is contrary to the Word of God, then he is a liar and God is true. **"God forbid: yea, let God be true, but every man a liar; as it is written, That thou mightest be justified in thy** sayings, and mightest overcome when thou art judged" (Romans 3:4). Therefore, I was not sold on the doctor's report. "Whose report shall you believe, Ye shall believe the report of the Lord" (Isaiah 53:1). Yes, I was being a real trooper, faith strong, and determined. Can I tell you, this was not just my test, it was also a test for my siblings. My two sisters and my brother were informed that it was highly likely they too had colorectal cancer. This thing was hereditary — genetically passed on!

It was years later at a family reunion that we learned we had inherited a horrible family trait from my father's side of the family. This was discovered because I thought it only fair to inform my cousins, uncles, and aunts who attended the reunion on what we learned so that they too could get examined. I had intentions on informing my relatives on my mother's side as well. Unbeknownst to me and my sisters, we learned we had lost several relatives on my father's side from the same disease (formal name: familial adenomatous polyposis).

Unfortunately, "back in the day," relatives did not talk about what a person in the family died from. The cause of death of a relative seemed to be taboo. This is so unfair for the future generations. We need to understand that panicking and hiding facts from family members is unhelpful. It is so important to know medical history. For example, when a woman is pregnant, her gynecologist will ask for family medical history so it would be known what to look for in the patient and the unborn baby so that proper medical care can be provided.

Also, in my case, if this knowledge of colorectal cancer had been passed down, I would have gotten examined before I turned forty! This knowledge could have prevented me from having to go through multiple surgeries. Early detection is the key to a longer life.

Many of you may know the well-known beginning of a holiness testimony: "If it was not for the Lord on my side, where would I be?" Now, please do not misinterpret my thinking. I believe that there is a purpose for everything that God allows and there are things we must struggle through. For if we do not go through the struggles, how would we get to know God?

Through every trial, tribulation, or storm that we experience in life, God will turn it around and make a blessing out of it. Our difficult times and challenges that we walk through can bring glory to Him. God will use our life experiences, whether they be joyous or sad, and turn them around to draw and encourage others to Him. This turn around helps us to remember that "it's not what it looks like" and what we see around us is not all there is. God has more in store for us, so believe that "greater or better is coming." Trust in Him! Have faith in Him! Continue to pray!

As difficult as it is, we must include in our prayers, "Lord, thy will be done." I know, it is hard when you're in one of those challenging situations, whether it is a medical, legal, or financial test. Yes, I said test. I view each of my challenges as a test of my faith. In the Bible, James says: **"My brethren, count it all joy when ye fall into divers temptations; Knowing this, that the trying of your faith worketh patience. But let patience have her perfect work, that ye may be perfect and entire, wanting nothing"** **(James 1:2-4).** So, in other words, count it joy whenever you face trouble or adversities because when you are tested, your faith produces perseverance. Because you hung in there, you matured and are complete, lacking for nothing. He is not referring to our immediate response to a situation but rather how we label that situation when we analyze our entire lives. Therefore, I knew my faith would be stronger and I would be a better person for it.

It was not only a test for me and my siblings but also my mother. How can a mother go through such a thing where all four of her children would have to endure such challenging situations simultaneously? My mother loved us so much that she would do almost anything to help us. She was there for all of us, through thick and thin. My mother's love was unconditional; no strings attached. Mom loved us for who we are and did not look for anything in return. Anyone who knew my mom, knew about all of us, too. Yes, she had bragging rights. She was a proud mother, and rightfully so. She raised four children by herself after Dad's death and provided love, security, nurturing and a loving home. Mom was very protective and unyielding when it came to her children. She was a strong woman, a strong mother, and a God-fearing woman.

A month had passed, and it was time for my colonoscopy. My nerves were shot while waiting for the prep for general anesthesia. It was not so much the prepping but more so the results that made me apprehensive and nervous. As I lay on the hospital bed, I began to pray inwardly. My stomach was in knots. Wesley was with me, and I did not want him to know how nervous I was. We made small talk to pass time as we waited. When the time came, Wesley was escorted to the waiting area and the anesthesia was then administered intravenously. It was the best sleep that I had in an awfully long time. I did not want to wake up. Slowly, the anesthesia wore off, and realization of the reason why I was there came to me. Wesley was called back to be with me and while we waited, we noticed the gastroenterologist doctor just kept pacing and walking by us. As he did this, he would look at me and walk away. We thought this was rather strange and became extremely nervous at this point.

Finally, the gastroenterologist, who performed the colonoscopy, summoned us into his office. Obviously, he found it difficult to tell a young forty-year-old woman that she had colorectal cancer and that my large intestine was completely infested with polyps of all sizes. Oh, and by the way, there also appears to be one nasty looking polyp that most likely was cancerous.

Upon hearing this devastating report, I could hear the rampant pounding of my heart. My hands trembled, and chills ran up and down my spine as though a cold breeze entered the room. My arms were coated with goosebumps. This was the first time I had any real health issue. I was completely stunned. As sweat beaded down my face, I was ready to dash out of the doctor's office. Wesley looked me straight in the eyes and reached for my clammy hands. His big strong hands cupped my hands. I knew then that we were in this together, through thick and thin. We both were determined to remain calm for the duration of the report. We had no idea of what lay ahead.

The gastroenterologist referred me to a colorectal surgeon. All three doctors, the gynecologist, gastroenterologist, and colorectal surgeon, were conveniently located in the same vicinity which made it easy to visit. Wesley and I felt comfortable knowing the doctors were affiliated with the same hospital. We were scheduled for a consultation in November 1999, with the colorectal surgeon who seemed to be somewhat distant. I do not want to use the word cold but perhaps he would be better described as not being a people person.

We sat in the amazingly comfortable, but small, office. The colorectal surgeon was seated at a desk along one wall, his black chair turned toward his computer as he slowly punched one key at a time. He then turned to us, greeting us cordially. Ten minutes into our visit, he began giving us his professional background. Next, it was my turn for yet another examination. It was not another colonoscopy but rather a rectal examination. After the examination, I began to get somewhat emotional.

The colorectal surgeon was giving me so many details on what steps he was going to take and how he was going to perform this major and difficult surgery. He pulled out a diagram of a human and began pointing to various areas of the body.

It was as if I was listening to a horror story. The colorectal surgeon seemed to be enjoying his presentation and proud of his ability to be able to perform such a surgery. Again, things really got to be too much for me to handle. He told us, "I'm sorry to have to tell you this but these are the cards that were dealt to you," and "I don't know what I'm going to find when I get inside." Did I hear him correctly?

It seemed as though I was in a cave as the words echoed in my ears. My mind began to race with questions like, did this cancer spread throughout my body? Was this cancer killing me? Am I going to live? Wesley was holding my sweaty hands trying to give me comfort. After what seemed like hours, I tried to digest what we were just informed. My mind began to race again. I could not focus enough to pray! I began to perspire — this time I was perspiring profusely.

Suddenly, I could not hear what the colorectal surgeon was saying though his mouth was moving. Like a robot, I stood up, put on my coat, and announced that I had had enough and that we were leaving. Wesley begged me to stay. I just could not take it any longer; the information was too overbearing. I could not tolerate hearing negative news from what I thought was an insensitive doctor. As we began to leave, the colorectal surgeon responded in a soft but firm voice, "Well, I cannot perform the surgery until I inform you of everything that the surgery entails!" Needless to say, we left anyway. Wesley pleaded with me once we were in the elevator, but I just was not ready to continue to hear the gory details. I was trying to cope with the fact that this was really happening to me. *My God, I am only forty and I am going through this, what they call an old person's disease!*

To think that I thought that having a cesarean was the worst thing that could happen to me. Having a cesarean was a piece of cake or a walk in the park compared to what the colorectal surgeon was telling me. I wanted to run from it all; just me running away like a scared cat or animal. Running for my life, away from this horrible nightmare. I cried and cried some more as we took the long and speechless walk to the car. Once we were in the car, my senses slowly began to come back. I prayed and prayed. I prayed some more. Still, I prayed. I never questioned God on why this was happening to me. I began to dig deep and search within myself, trying to figure out if I had done something wrong in my life to be handed such horrible news.

At this point, I literally had to get ahold of myself because I was heading into the guilt and blame game. Warning, this is not the path you want to take. Self-blame is toxic. The fact is, we are human beings and therefore, we make mistakes. What is dangerous is that we think we are right all the time, but we cannot dwell in that delusional state. Mistakes happen and we need to take responsibility and do what we can to correct the problem. Pray about it and move on. In my opinion, the stress was growing, causing me to feel guilty and blame myself for my body's imperfections; I was determined not to stay in this frame of mind. Though my body's imperfection was not my fault, I decided to take responsibility and have the problem corrected.

A few days passed and I began to accept what God allowed. I accepted that this was not going to be an easy path, and this was a life and death situation. The only choice I had was to contact the surgeon and complete the consultation. After all, if I did not do anything, the cancer would take over my body and win. I am not a quitter or loser. God cannot fail me. I contacted the colorectal surgeon and set another appointment a few weeks after the initial consultation.

Through much prayer and support from Wesley and family I went to the surgeon alone. By the way, I never shared with my family on how I performed at the surgeon's office nor the fact that I was simply afraid. Everyone viewed me as this strong faithful God-fearing Christian woman. Let me encourage you today. You do not have to be strong all the time. We are human and thus have emotions and feelings. It is important and healthy for us to release those emotions and fears. It is OK to be afraid but know that God is in control.

CHAPTER 3

The Power of Hope

The day of my second consultation, I went to work. Keeping busy kept my nerves together and my mind off what I was about to face. I told Wesley I could handle the consultation alone, but I was not alone; I had God on my side. Yes, my faith had stepped up. My faith was always there but the human part had a little upper hand, if only just for a moment. I knew with the grace of God I could handle this.

It was late November, and the weather was a bit chilly, but at least we had not received any snow. As I walked the five blocks to the colorectal surgeon's office for my consultation, I prayed The Lord's Prayer out loud. I did not care who heard me. I was going into battle! I was mentally dressed for war with the six armors of God found in **Ephesians 6:10-18** — my sword of the spirit, the belt of truth, breastplate of righteousness, shoes of the gospel, shield of faith, and helmet of salvation — not to hurt him, but to demolish that air of arrogance or overbearing confidence or control that the colorectal surgeon may have thought he had over me. My thoughts were to not believe that my life was over, but to continue to do my best to live upright and be transparent, honest and know the greatness of God.

This time, my wall was not going to crumble; it was going to be the other way around. I felt like I was in battle, and not in fear, for my wall was protected. God and I were going to tear down the colorectal surgeon's wall — his wall of "I'm in Control."

Finally, I reached the building and took the elevator up to the 4th floor. After exhaling, I felt at ease and determined not to lose control of my emotions. My breathing flowed at a steady rate. We were ready for battle.

The consultation was completely different than the first. I entered the office with a smile and took a seat. The colorectal surgeon had a look of surprise on his face. I knew he expected me to cry like before. What he did not know was that Grace and Mercy were sitting right next to me, metaphorically speaking, and that I was already claiming the victory.

God is faithful and just. I thank God for his Grace and Mercy, which work hand in hand. God will forgive our sins if we confess our transgressions to Him. God cancels out our sin so that we are free and unbounded to love Him. All debts of sin are canceled out. We serve a forgiving God, unlike man who never forgets your past. The Bible reassures us with the scripture that says: **"He hath not dealt with us after our sins; nor rewarded us according to our iniquities. For as the heaven is high above the earth, so great is his mercy toward them that fear him. As far as the east is from the west, so far hath he removed our transgressions from us"** **(Psalm 103:10-12).** So, yes, I am a child of God, and my faith is strong. After all, God promised to give us the desires of our heart;

mine being healing. **"Delight thyself also in the LORD: and he shall give thee the desires of thine heart" (Psalm 37:4).**

Through prayer and God's Grace and Mercy, God can heal in an instant! **"But He was wounded for our transgressions. He was bruised for our iniquities; The chastisement for our peace was upon Him, And by His stripes we are healed" (Isaiah 53:5).** My surgery date was set for December 1999. Once the surgery date was set, I must admit, I wondered whether I would live to see the "big" celebration of the new year. Then I thought, *Whatever God's will, it shall be done.* I was appreciative that, at least, we did get a chance to celebrate my 41st birthday in November, though it was somewhat somber, knowing the surgery date was fast approaching.

It had now been a couple of weeks after my consultation with the colorectal surgeon. Wesley and I were at home sitting comfortably in the kitchen watching television when the doorbell rang. Oh no, we completely forgot that we had an appointment with a representative from a cemetery and crematory company. Can you believe, at such a time in my life, we were having a meeting about death? Was this a confirmation from God that my life would soon be over? The timing seemed uncanny. We guided him to our dining room table where he laid out his presentation material. Wesley looked at me as if to say, "This is going to be a long meeting." And I was thinking, no way did I want to have this discussion.

Needless to say, the meeting was cut short, not only because of my medical situation or fear, but the fact that the representative was pushing us to take out a loan for burial expenses. We were financially capable of paying in full, but he kept trying to persuade us to take out a loan. It just did not seem feasible for us to pay interest on something that was not necessary, at least I hoped neither one of us would need a burial site anytime soon. We told the representative, "Good night," and "No thank you." And with that, the meeting was over.

***

It is not easy for any family to hear of a loved one's diagnosis with any type of disease. Colorectal cancer, like other cancers and mental illnesses, carries a stigma of a dim outcome. These are terrible diseases that bring terror to the person who has them and to their loved ones. People immediately view these diseases as a death sentence. Nevertheless, there is always hope. Research continues to be done, including genealogy research, in which I declined to participate. It was not the right time for me, as I was focused on tackling my situation first.

Support from family and friends is so important when you are going through trials and tribulations. These are times when you find out who really loves and cares for you. I was blessed as I had so much support. My friends prayed with and for me, as did my family members.

I was at peace with having surgery, or so I thought. I began having two specific dreams. One dream was of a fine misty rain falling from the clear blue sky. It would fall on a huge open hole in the roof of a building. I always had a desire to rent out houses. Therefore, I assume I owned this building or home that was in my dream. It was so vivid.

I needed a roofer to repair the hole in the roof. I told a person who appeared in my dream that it had to be an Italian guy because he did fantastic masonry and roofing work. There was never a conclusion on whether the roofer repaired the hole because my dream ended.

The second repetitive dream was of small children sleeping in my attic. There were rows and rows of beds that had white wrought-iron bed frames with white sheets. All the children were dressed in pure white nightgowns, and there was a man standing by the pool. Each child appeared to be ready to be baptized.

A close girlfriend of mine, a prophetess, interpreted these dreams for me. The dream of the misty rain was the sign that my body was going to go through a washing or a cleansing from the poison that was inside my body, which was the heavily infested large intestine and the cancerous polyp. The hole in the roof signified that there was going to be repairs on the outside of my body that would need closure.

The second dream, with the children, was that I was being baptized, going to be renewed, refreshed, and re-born after undergone surgery.

How many of you readers know that Jesus washes away your sins and the blood of Jesus makes you white as snow? Spiritually, snow is a symbol of purity, cleanliness, and righteousness. The scriptures in the **Book of Isaiah** say, in **Chapter 1:18, "Come now, and let us reason together, saith the Lord: though your sins be as scarlet, they shall be as white as snow; though they be red like crimson, they shall be as wool."** The washing away of our sins is the concept that all our sins can be forgiven by God. In His eyes, we are clear and free from our sins if we accept Jesus as our Lord and Savior. Sin is unclean, and to enter the Kingdom of God or be in God's presence, all dirt (sin) must be washed away. Thank you, Jesus, for the blood! Praise God for the blood of Jesus! For it is through His blood that we might be saved. It is by the blood of Jesus that our sins are cast away and forgotten.

Our sins are called out for what they are — sins. We are given the chance to give up our violent, cruel, distasteful, sinful ways. At times, I am sure you sit at home thinking about things that you have done wrong and/or things that you might have said that hurt someone's feelings. Man does not forget, but be at peace knowing that God forgives. When you come to know the Lord for yourself, you will be comforted to know that he cares and loves us unconditionally.

I want to talk a little about dreams and visions. God will communicate to us by way of dreams and visions. Visions from God convey revelations that can amaze you. I viewed my dreams as revelation or confirmation that I would come out of this ordeal like new. As a Christian, we are called to bring God glory through hardships. In the book of **Genesis**, Joseph interpreted the dreams of the butler and baker of the king of Egypt.

> **"1) And it came to pass after these things, that the butler of the king of Egypt and his baker had offended their lord the king of Egypt. ... 5) And they dreamed a dream both of them, each man his dream in one night, each man according to the interpretation of his dream, the butler and the baker of the king of Egypt, which were bound in the prison.... 9) And the chief butler told his dream to Joseph, and said to him, In my dream, behold, a vine was before me; 10) And in the vine were three branches: and it was as though it budded, and her blossoms shot forth; and the clusters thereof brought**

forth ripe grapes: 11) And Pharaoh's cup was in my hand: and I took the grapes, and pressed them into Pharaoh's cup, and I gave the cup into Pharaoh's hand.... 16) When the chief baker saw that the interpretation was good, he said unto Joseph, I also was in my dream, and, behold, I had three white baskets on my head: 17) And in the uppermost basket there was of all manner of bakemeats for Pharaoh; and the birds did eat them out of the basket upon my head. 18) And Joseph answered and said, This is the interpretation thereof: The three baskets are three days: 19) Yet within three days shall Pharaoh lift up thy head from off thee, and shall hang thee on a tree; and the birds shall eat thy flesh from off thee. 20) And it came to pass the third day, which was Pharaoh's birthday, that he made a feast unto all his servants: and he lifted up the head of the chief butler and of the chief baker among his servants. 21) And he restored the chief butler unto his butlership again; and he gave the cup into Pharaoh's hand: 22) But he hanged the chief baker: as Joseph had interpreted to them" (Genesis 40:1-22).

Remember, my siblings also had the same diagnosis except for the stage of cancer — I was in Stage 4. None of their polyps seemed to be cancerous. It was decided that we would handle the required surgeries one person at a time. Me, of course, being the first, since I was in what we thought was the worst shape. To prepare myself for surgery, praying became a non-stop "ritual" by the saints and myself. We prayed with expectation. I resolved to the fact that this is what God had for me and I had faith that the healing was going to be my testimony. According to **Isaiah 53:5: "But he was wounded for our transgressions, he was bruised for our iniquities: the chastisement of our peace was upon him; and with his stripes we are healed."** After all, the worst thing that happened surgically to me was having a cesarean birth. After this, there will be a renewed, refreshed and re-born me.

In December 1999, I was ready for my surgery. The object of the surgery, called a colectomy, was to remove my large intestine (the colon) and whatever else the colorectal surgeon found that might put me in danger. The colon is part of the digestive system. The colorectal surgeon was not sure whether he would need to remove all or part of the colon. If part of the colon was to be removed, then the remaining sections would be reconnected to the rectum to allow waste to escape from the body. If the entire colon was to be removed, then I would have an ostomy and need to wear an ostomy bag. The surgery was to last 4–6 hours. It lasted 6 hours.

Prayers from those who my mother told were being sent up. My friends were praying for me. Wesley, my sisters, and my brother were praying for me. This is the first time any one of us had to undergo major surgery. My girlfriend, the prophetess who interpreted my dreams prior, came up to the hospital, along with my family and a friend of the family, to pray with me before the surgery.

My girlfriend, the prophetess, prayed a mighty prayer and said prior to the prayer in a soft but stern voice, "If there is anyone in this room that is not serious, get out now." I thought, *Oh my, watch out Satan, the chief warrior is in this room.* Well, if that did not get me to be strong, nothing else would. After her mighty, awesome, tear-jerking prayer, I was again ready for battle. I hugged my family and felt the love that was evident from each one who was in the room. I knew then that God was not going to allow me to leave them yet.

The orderly came in the room and called my name. He asked me to confirm my birth date and name. I was ready. Here we go, Lord! As the orderly rolled me down the halls of the hospital and to the operating room, I was saying, you got it, "The Lord's Prayer." I told myself, "Don't fear, for the Lord thy God got me." And I remembered that God said, "He would never leave me nor forsake me." I am your child and you, Father God, promised You would give me the desires of my heart. **Hebrews 13:5 "…for he hath said, I will never leave thee, nor forsake thee."**

God does not go back on His word, unlike man. We often say, "A promise is a promise." But we all know what it is like when a promise is broken. You may feel disappointed, dismayed, hurt and no longer have faith or trust in a person. God does not break His promises. **Isaiah 41:10** reads as such: **"Fear thou not; for I am with thee: be not dismayed; for I am thy God: I will strengthen thee; yea, I will help thee; yea, I will uphold thee with the right hand of my righteousness."** And therefore, I put my trust in Him. **"Trust in him at all times; ye people, pour out your heart before him: God is a refuge for us. Selah" (Psalm 62:8).** God is a guiding light. We see best in the light versus the limited sight in darkness. God is a source of goodness, purity, and holiness. While spiritually, darkness is evil. **"Thy word is a lamp unto my feet, and a light unto my path" (Psalm 119:105).**

I do not recall much else once the general anesthesia took complete control over my body. I awoke in my hospital bed alone except for the other patient in the room. What!!?? I did not have my own room. No, but seriously, that did not bother me, not one bit. The very first thing I did was feel my stomach area. You are probably wondering, why? I was feeling to see whether I had a colostomy bag attached to my body.

Thank you, Jesus! **Hallelujah!** There was no big lump under the sheets; therefore, no colostomy bag attached to my body. The colorectal surgeon had performed a subtotal colectomy with ileorectal anastomosis — partial colon removal. There was no question on whether chemotherapy was an option as part of my recovery plan, which consisted of six months with three hours of chemo treatment on a weekly basis.

Once I was released from the hospital and homeward bound, I felt so blessed that the colorectal surgeon did not remove my entire colon. However, my middle sister, Jan, was totally upset with the surgeon. She knew that I would require another surgery to remove the remaining part of my colon. Jan talked to the surgeon to get his reasoning on the decision he made. His response was that he could not see me coping with both the colostomy bag and getting chemotherapy. It was a decision that he made while in the middle of the surgery and, therefore, he would perform a second surgery.

As for my feelings, I think the surgeon made the right decision. I figured that since the worst section of the colon was removed, I had plenty of time before I needed the second surgery. I did not think about the fact that my entire colon was infested with polyps, and polyps grow! Hmmm, looking back at the situation, perhaps the colorectal surgeon should have removed the entire colon. I think he reflected on how I reacted initially in his office when he related the information on how and what was going to be done at my surgery. As the saying goes, "First impressions stick."

I began receiving my chemotherapy treatments at a clinic not far from the hospital where I had my surgery. Fortunately for Wesley, my mother-in-law also had her chemotherapy treatments at the same clinic. Therefore, he could take the two of us to our appointments together if they were scheduled on the same day and time. When my mother-in-law found out we had our treatments at the same clinic, she sounded excited. I am not so sure why, because I took my having to have treatments very personal. I can only assume that my mother-in-law felt we had more in common. But for me, this was very private, and I did not feel comfortable going to the clinic with anyone who had to be treated for cancer. It was not a joyous occasion. Or was it because I was in denial and believed my chemo treatments were just for precautionary steps? I simply did not want to be in this situation; I hated having to go through this.

My mother-in-law was diagnosed with melanoma skin cancer after she first noticed as a dark, completely round spot on the bottom of her foot. Melanoma, for those of you who don't know, according to Webster's Dictionary, is "an aggressive **cancer** that tends to metastasize relatively early and aggressively, thereby spreading to other parts of the body. These **cancers** may be fatal if not found and treated early." Wesley agreed that it was convenient to take both of us versus having to drive us individually to our separate appointments.

I cannot imagine how Wesley felt, having to cope with two women who he loved who were dealing with some form of cancer; both cancers were considered life-threatening. I know that God will not put on us more than we can handle, but I know Wesley had to feel overwhelmed and fearful for both me and his mother. He never talked to me about his feelings but would only say, "We will get through this together."

My son, Stephen, would assure me that I was going to be alright. He supported me as much as he could; always checking up on Mommy. Wesley showed his support by continuing to do the housework, though he had always helped around the house. He cooked perfect meals. Of course, my taste for food had left me and was replaced by a metal-like taste when I ate after having chemotherapy.

The chemotherapy clinic representative called to check on me after my first couple of treatments. I told her I was feeling great as I was determined that the treatments were not going to bother me one bit! I am sure I sounded a little indignant to her with my response. But boy did the treatments hit me like a ton of bricks after the second dose.

I had to have three-hour treatments once a week for six months. It was as if the chemotherapy sapped the strength right from under my feet and knocked the wind out of me. It was like a wave of heaviness that laid upon my eyes and my brain. I would sleep for what seemed like 10 minutes when, really, I slept through the entire night. Still, I managed to get up, get dressed and go to work. Feeling exhausted had become a norm for me.

When I returned home from work, I did not want to eat, talk, or do anything. I only wanted to crawl into bed and fall asleep, and that is just want I did. The treatments were getting the best of me. My hands and lips became dry and cracked, which was a little painful. The pigmentation of my skin became darker, as though I had been sitting in the beautiful, warm sun. I really had not noticed, until one of my co-workers commented on how radiant my complexion was and asked where I went to get my tan. That is when I took notice by staring at myself in the mirror. I realized that, not only did my complexion get darker, my hands, lips and my baby toes became dark, too. My baby toe was so dark that I took a sewing needle and stabbed it to ensure that the nerves were intact. Yep, the nerves were still working, ouch!

I soon realized that driving to appointments for my mother-in-law and me was getting to be too much for Wesley. That is when I made the decision to have my chemotherapy treatments at home. I also did not like hearing nor seeing other patients at the clinic physically getting sick from their treatments. It was getting to be too much for me. I recall seeing a TV personality there with what I think was a close friend. Evidently, her treatment caused her to lose her hair. I know this because she wore a red bandana on her head. She looked very pale and sickly. They were moved to a private room. I wondered how I, too, could get my own private room. Later, I found out that it was on a first come, first serve basis. I never got a private room, which helped me decide to have treatments at home. Again, it was not in my best interest to see other people coping with their cancer and getting sick. It impacted me negatively. God help me!

When you call on the Lord, He hears you. You just do not know when He is going to answer. I continued calling on the Lord. I needed His help and guidance. I never gave up hope, and

I tried to embrace what God obviously intended for me to go through. I continued to encourage myself with these Bible scriptures and many others:

> **Isaiah 41:10 – Fear thou not; for I [am] with thee: be not dismayed; for I [am] thy God: I will strengthen thee; yea, I will help thee; yea, I will uphold thee with the right hand of my righteousness.**
>
> **Hebrews 13:5 – [Let your] conversation [be] without covetousness; and be content with such things as ye have: for he hath said, I will never leave thee, nor forsake thee.**
>
> **Deuteronomy 31:6 – Be strong and of a good courage, fear not, nor be afraid of them: for the LORD thy God, he it is that doth go with thee; he will not fail thee, nor forsake thee.**
>
> **Romans 8:28 – And we know that all things work together for good to them that love God, to them who are the called according to his purpose.**
>
> **2 Timothy 1:7 – For God hath not given us the spirit of fear; but of power, and of love, and of a sound mind.**
>
> **1 Peter 5:7 – Casting all your care upon him; for he careth for you.**

Making the decision for treatments at home meant that many, many boxes of medical supplies arrived at our house. The boxes were stored in our dining room. It also meant that a nurse would need to arrive at my house at 7am the day before I was to receive my treatments to get my blood for bloodwork for the lab. It had to be 7am sharp because I was still going into the office. I would complain whenever the nurse was late because she was making me late. When I look back at it now, how absurd it was of me to get angry whenever she arrived late. She was helping me live, and I had an attitude?!

Wesley seemed fine with me having treatments at home. However, as time passed, I thought about how our son Stephen was taking all of this. To see the medical supplies and a nurse coming to give me my treatments in the evenings once a week for three hours had to affect him. I did not like our son having the visual of me getting chemotherapy. He would go upstairs to his room while the nurse would sit with me and administer my chemo. I also did not like seeing all the medical supplies stored in our dining room, because it began to look like a hospital. No, this cannot be good for our son. There were other negative consequences of having my chemo treatments at home.

I felt like I had to entertain the nurse for those three hours of treatment. We would try to talk for the three hours, but, of course, I would fall asleep at each visit. Her visits began to become annoying to me because: 1) She began asking for green tea and where is my teapot — she had to prepare it herself because I was completely drained. This meant she had to have access to my kitchen and search around for what she needed. 2) My veins began to collapse from getting so many needles and she said she was getting tired of trying to get my veins to "pop up." We would try running cold water on my arms, "smacking" my arms, and of course, tying the band around my arm was no longer working. She recommended I get a stent put in. 3) She told me, in so many words, that I probably would not make it because this type of cancer was a killer.

I had enough of the nurse and home treatments. I was not going to get a stent put in. A stent is a like a tube placed temporarily in a blood vessel that would help relieve a blockage or obstruction that was preventing the needle from being inserted in my arm. A stent meant that it would become easier for the nurse to give me my chemo because she would no longer need to stick me with a needle. Sounds perfect, right? Well, not for me. I did not want another cut or scar on me. I had enough stitches and scars on me to last a lifetime. I know, I was not acting nice. It was not that I was being vain, but rather I was overwhelmed and just plain old tired of going through this.

I prayed more and more as I could see the negative way I was behaving and how my treatments at home were affecting our son. I do not think my behavior, denial and anger, was from the chemo, but rather from the entire medical ordeal.

The effects of receiving chemotherapy made me sleepy, like I had been given a sedative. A cold, then a burning sensation flowed through my veins, and the feeling of nausea and loss of appetite came with each treatment. The treatments also gave me a metal-like taste in my mouth, skin discoloration, dry cracked hands and extreme fatigue.

Chemotherapy affects every cell in your body, both good and bad. I had no hair loss, but if I did, my two sisters said that they would shave their heads in support of me. It was a show of their love for me, and they did not want me to feel alone in this walk. There is nothing like sisterly love!

My instructions after each treatment were to drink plenty of water or any kind of liquids, like soup or popsicles, to help prevent dehydration, and help wash out toxins from the body. During my weekly visits to the oncologist, he would have me open my mouth to check for sores, check for weight loss and then would read my bloodwork results.

Wesley was my advocate and wanted, and needed, to be with me during my treatments. He continued to drive both me and my mother-in-law to our separate treatments. I know this had to be draining for him. I eventually told him it was no longer necessary to attend my bloodwork appointments nor my follow-ups with the oncologist. I had concern for Wesley and wanted him to be able to work and not worry about me going to my treatments. It was important for things to be as normal as possible. After three months, I had begun to feel that I could get home by myself after my chemo treatments. After all, I had gone back to work, and the clinic was within walking distance from my office. I received my chemo every Friday at 4pm. My strength would come back by Thursday, just in time for the next round. It was a vicious cycle. When would normality return in our life?

While recuperating at home, Wesley received a call from the colorectal surgeon. They had a somewhat brief conversation. I sat looking at Wesley, wondering why he had a perplexing look on his face. He sat beside me and held my hand. I was thinking, *Oh no, we got horrible news about the results of my surgery!* Beads of sweat appeared on my forehead. As the sweat rolled down into my eyes, they began to burn; tears were also rolling down my cheeks, and a knot rose in my throat. My heart began to race, and I wanted to scream at him. Instead, I yelled, saying, "Oh God, what is going on? Tell me now!"

"Calm down," was Wesley's response. He said, "There is nothing to worry about, but..."

I interrupted him by saying, "But what?!"

He responded, "Honey, remember when the colorectal surgeon did the rectal examination in his office? Well, you and I both forgot that he mentioned that there were polyps in your rectum that needed to be removed." Right! At the time we were told this, it was such a minor surgery, considering what we were told would take place for the main surgery. Therefore, we completely forgot about it.

As I calmed down, we hugged each other as tears rolled down my face. I felt awful for yelling at my sweet, adorable, handsome husband. He sat me down on our paisley, burgundy-colored comfortable sofa and waited for my breathing to become normal. Wesley looked at me lovingly and told me everything would be all right. I believed him, and most of all, I believed God would take care of this, too.

This surgery was going to be easy and there would be no visible scars. The procedure was an out-patient surgery. In the month of January 2000, Wesley and I drove to the out-patient area located in a different building than the hospital. As I prepared myself, Wesley waited in the waiting area. I prayed and prayed. I felt confident and knew that everything was going to be all right, and I would walk out from the surgery fine.

In the small, cold operating room, I lay on my stomach, thinking how embarrassing this was, but it was necessary. This time, the colorectal surgeon, the same surgeon who removed my colon, seemed more pleasant. We even talked a little. Shortly, as I was praying, the anesthesiologist came in and prepped me, and within seconds, I felt light-headed. I was out like a lightbulb. I do not recall getting dressed but I do recall our ride home. The anesthesia began wearing off and I started feeling a slight burning sensation in my buttocks. I thought, *Hmm, nothing that I cannot bear.*

We arrived home and I went straight to bed, with pain medication, of course. The pain had gotten worse. Two days later, it was time for my chemotherapy treatment. During my treatment, I could feel the cold liquid flowing through my veins and I think with the chemo treatments, the chemo medicine must have trickled down in the surgical area, thus causing a fiery, burning sensation. All I could do was pray. "Lord, please give me some comfort through this storm. Deliver me from this pain—take the pain away." I just called out to the Lord, and at many times, simply called out His name: "Jesus, Jesus, Jesus." I know you, Lord, have a purpose for my life. I believe there is more for me to do. The written word says, **"Grant thee according to thine own heart, and fulfil all thy counsel" (Psalm 20:4).** God has a purpose for us all and believing this gave me the strength to push through this storm.

Sometimes, a person can be in so much pain that all they can do is call on the Name of Jesus! I am sure you have been there, too. There is power in the name of Jesus. There is strength in the name of Jesus. Jesus is a protector. The written word says, **"The LORD is my rock, and my fortress, and my deliverer; my God, my strength, in whom I will trust; my buckler, and the horn of my salvation, and my high tower" (Psalm 18:2).** I strongly believed that our life would return to normal because Jesus can heal the sick. **Matthew 15:21-28** speaks about a Gentile woman's plea for help to heal her sick daughter. In verse 28 it says: **"Then Jesus answered and said unto her, O woman, great is thy faith: be it unto thee even as thou wilt. And her daughter was made whole from that very hour."** It also says that the daughter was healed in that same hour.

There are many verses in the Bible that give us knowledge of Jesus' power to heal. Jesus healed the lame, blind, mute, maimed and so on. Jesus touched two blind men's eyes, and immediately they received their sight, and they followed Him. **"And as they departed from Jericho, a great multitude followed him. And, behold, two blind men sitting by the way side, when they heard that Jesus passed by, cried out, saying, Have mercy on us, O Lord, thou son of David. And the multitude rebuked them, because they should hold their peace: but they cried the more, saying, Have mercy on us, O Lord, thou son of David. And Jesus stood still, and called them, and said, What will ye that I shall do unto you? They say unto him, Lord, that our eyes may be opened. So Jesus had compassion on them, and touched their eyes: and immediately their eyes received sight, and they followed him"** (Matthew 20:29-34). Who would not want to follow Jesus after that? I am following Jesus because He is my savior. Jesus healed "great multitudes." Surely, He can heal me too.

CHAPTER 4

Trials Plus Tribulations Equals Triumph

As time passed, Wesley and I continued to work at our respective jobs. Stephen went to his high school in Center City and seemed to be coping well. His grades were average, unlike during middle and grade school where he excelled. I could only assume that, just like most teenage boys, he felt that he no longer needed Mommy's input or directions. After all, he was now in high school and could stand on his own. How wrong was he?

I continued with my six months of chemotherapy and was very anxious to finish. The treatments were draining me. My mother-in-law's cancer advanced and she now was on experimental cancer medications. She continued to have a positive attitude and so did Wesley.

As time progressed, so did my mother-in-law's cancer. The cancer was not only in her foot, where it was originally spotted, but had metastasized throughout her body. We continued to be prayerful and hopeful that she would get through it. My prayer

51

was that God could still fix it. From what I recall, she was prescribed various chemo medicines to fight the cancer. Through it all, she continued to be strong and enjoyed life. She even went on vacation. She never complained about pain nor about her condition. She was an inspiration to me during my time of chemotherapy.

My six months of chemotherapy treatments were finally over. I was so jubilant and could not wait for normalcy to return to my life. I worked diligently and decided to continue furthering my education. I registered for two courses at Widener University, one on Tuesday evenings and the other on Saturday mornings. I knew I had to manage my time, so I prepared several dinners for the week on Saturday afternoons. I wanted to ensure that my hubby and son could not complain about not having dinner prepared.

It took some strategy on my part to be able to keep up with house chores and plan time to study. I was determined to get my life back on track. I continued singing and being the assistant directress at my church. Also, I went back to working with the children at my church, who were so glad to see me return. I recall one child was so happy to see me at church, she ran towards me, right smack dab into my stomach. My mother was standing next to me, and she grabbed me as I doubled over in pain. The little girl was frightened and did not understand that my stomach was still tender after having major surgery. It was all so innocent. I stood up and gave her a gentle hug, ensuring her that I was fine.

My energy level increased as time passed. My enthusiasm to walk that Godly walk increased. As you may have experienced, when you have been through a traumatic, life-threatening situation, you get a different perspective on life. Remember earlier

I said I felt renewed, refreshed and reborn. Yes, I felt like a new person, appreciative of every little thing life had to offer me. There would be no complaints from me.

There were times when I would just sit by our kitchen patio, looking out and admiring the wondrous work of God. I was admiring the colorful trees during the fall, watching the colorful leaves fall from the trees, and watching birds fly from tree to tree. The joyful sound of children playing in the driveway awakened me to the fact that life was good, and, "God is good all the time, and all the time, God is good." And my goodness, it is good to be alive!

When winter came, I marveled at the snow-covered trees and bushes. To see the blanket of snow across the lawn was such a beautiful sight. It is awesome to be able to see the marvels of God's miraculous works!

When you slow down, "reflection time" can make a big difference. Taking time to reflect is important in that it helps you to understand what God has done for you and remind you of His faithfulness. Reflection time allows us to remember that if God did it once, He will show up and can do it over and over again; He never changes. The scripture says, **"Jesus Christ, the same yesterday, and to day and for ever" (Hebrews 13:8).** Just think of how many times we go against the will of God, and yet He still forgives us. Just think about what an amazing, awesome and forgiving God we serve. We must fast and pray for it is through prayer and fasting that we can overcome our fears or ordeals. We must be and stay in the will of God. We must obey and be in alignment with God's will. Yes, it is a spiritual effort and may, at times, be difficult, but in the scope of things, it is a huge reward. God is greater than anything that we can imagine.

Nothing much changed at work. Going on business trips had become somewhat of a routine. On one of my business trips to Knoxville, TN, I had called home to see how things were going. When Wesley answered, his voice sounded strange. When I asked what was going on, he told me his mother had been hospitalized. I knew this was not good. I tried consoling him, but how could I when I was miles from home? I wanted to take the first plane back home, but he insisted on me staying; I had one more day remaining and then I would be home. I followed his wishes, but felt guilty because I wanted to be there for Wesley. The next day, I quickly ran through the training session, changed my plane ticket to an earlier flight, and headed home.

Wesley and I visited his mother the next day. She seemed fine and asked him to make her one of his "famous" egg salad sandwiches. We left the hospital and returned in about two hours with the egg salad sandwich. She enjoyed it and said it was his best. I had to try it, so I did. Ugh. I thought it was horrible, too much black pepper. But the most important thing is that she enjoyed it and her only son made it just for her! We talked with her and went home to get some rest. The call came around midnight. We both jumped up, hurriedly got dressed and sped to the hospital. Moments later, my mother-in-law got her wings. We both wept.

Life seemed so unfair. It was not about me; now, it was Wesley who was hurting and heartbroken. I wondered, when was the storm going to be over for us? I am faithful. I pray diligently not just for me but for others, too. *What am I doing wrong?* I thought. *Why so much pain? Lord, I am crying out to you. We need your help!* I comforted Wesley, assuring him that his mother was at peace and no longer suffering. Looking back at this statement, this is not what people want to hear when they have just lost a loved one. Grief affects everyone differently. I gave him his personal space to grieve. I needed to compose myself so that I could be strong for him. I sat in our reclining chair at home and began reading the Bible for strength and comfort.

In the book of **Matthew, Chapter 18**, Jesus speaks about Elijah coming first to restore all things, but that Elijah did come but they (man) did not know him and did whatever they wished. And now, the Son of Man was going to suffer at the hands of man. Jesus was saying that Elijah came in the form of John the Baptist, who the king beheaded at the request of Herodias' daughter (**Matthew 14:1-12**).

Jesus assured his disciples that they could not cure the man who had a son with epilepsy because of their unbelief. However, if only disciples had "faith as a mustard seed they could say to this mountain, 'Move from here to there,' and it will move, and nothing will be impossible for you" (**Matthew 17:14-21**). I believe that our outcome depends on our faith (belief in God's power), prayer and fasting, and by His Grace and Mercy we can be healed. We must depend on God's healing power and know that He is with us 24 hours a day, 7 days a week, 365 days a year.

Whatever you are going through, the Lord is with you. It is OK to cry because "weeping may endure for a night but joy cometh in the morning." Morning does not mean 6am or whatever time you get out of bed, but your morning is when you get relief from your pain, from your suffering, from your depression or whatever it is consuming you and keeping you from moving forward with your walk with God. Morning can be the time you get a revelation that everything is going to be all right. Morning is feeling God's power of strength to get through the difficult time. When things become overwhelming, or if you feel lost and need direction or guidance, try reading the Bible. It's the best book ever; it is a book of instructions on life.

I had faith that "better is coming" and when I prayed, I prayed with exceedingly high expectations. I believe that having faith is not enough to be saved; one must also repent. I make it a point of asking God for forgiveness of known and unknown things I have done or of any unclean or sinful thoughts. God wants to demonstrate His love and kindness through His blessings to us. He wants us to know that 'better is coming,' and for us to exceed a double inheritance, and therefore, I try to not concentrate on the negative, but rather keep moving with purpose.

"For your shame ye shall have double; and for confusion they shall rejoice in their portion: therefore in their land they shall possess the double: everlasting joy shall be unto them" (Isaiah 61:7). I encourage, or rather implore, you to read the Bible as it is the best book ever. The Bible "unlocks spiritual treasures," teaching the Word of God.

I know that I am not the only person who had many trials and tribulations. Many of you have gone through, or are currently going through, difficult times even as you read this book. But, what encouraged me as I struggled through my difficult periods, is remembering what Job (in the Bible) went through, and oftentimes I viewed myself as a "Jobette." No, I am not comparing myself to Job, but it was a revelation to me.

I reread the book of Job, who was loved by God and had calamities. So, who are we that we should not also be tested? Job suffered much but the Lord worked it out for him. He was upright and feared God. Job had a large family, seven sons and three daughters. He possessed hundreds of donkeys, oxen, and sheep. The Lord asked Satan, where did you come from? In so many words, Satan replied with something like, "I was looking to and fro on Earth." The Lord questioned whether Satan tried Job. The Lord knew Job was a blameless, upright man and allowed all that Job had, and gave Satan power to take it all away. But the Lord instructed Satan not to physically lay a hand on Job.

Job's character was attacked by Satan. Job lost his property and all his children died. Job did not sin or blame God. Understand that God had a hedge of protection around Job. The Lord gave power to Satan to allow destruction and death to Job's property and children. God allowed Satan to test Job. He remained faithful. Again, Satan went to and fro on Earth seeking to destroy whom he can. This time, when God spoke with Satan, God gave Satan power to attack Job's health. Satan thought that since Job lost his property and his children died, surely if Job's body were afflicted, Job would curse God for not protecting him. And so, Job's body was fully covered with painful boils. Job suffered so much that even Job's wife wanted him to curse God and die. The pain was so unbearable that Job cursed the day he was born. Job was very bitter to say the least.

For me, it is a lesson of faith, and to teach us that we too will be put through tests and have trials and tribulations, lose loved ones, be attacked in our imperfect body, perhaps lose jobs and such, but the question is, will you remain faithful and trust God's purpose? No test, no testimony. It is through Job's suffering that we learn that we have challenges and questions and struggle for faith and understanding. Job teaches us about patience and endurance. It also reminds us that God is compassionate and merciful. God healed Job and gave him twice as much as he lost. **"And the LORD turned the captivity of Job, when he prayed for his friends: also the LORD gave Job twice as much as he had before"** **(Job 42:10).** I encourage you to read or reread the Book of Job to better understand the purpose of his sufferings. Prayerfully, you will be encouraged to press on in your life, and continue to have faith and trust in God.

CHAPTER 5

Proving My Faith

I was feeling great, and life was slowly getting back to normal. I was back! Completely healed, no soreness, I felt super. My faith in God kept me going. Time was moving on. My job kept me busy, along with my classwork and my home and church life. Those who knew what I had gone through were amazed.

Now, it was time for both of my sisters to have their surgeries, and believe me, they had complications! My poor mother endured all the hurt and pain of seeing her girls suffer. I just cannot imagine what she must have been feeling. We know Mom prayed for us daily! Her favorite saying was, "I won't complain."

Jan's surgery was about a month before Lin's. Jan's surgery required her to have her entire large intestine (colon) removed due to having multiple large tumors on the colon. Therefore, it would be required for her to wear an ostomy bag. Jan had her surgery in Philadelphia, with the same surgeon I had, so we knew the surgeon knew what he was doing. I say this because Jan had complications after her surgery.

The colorectal surgeon was baffled and could not understand why she could not hold or swallow her own saliva. She would vomit and spit constantly in a container. She had to always keep the container by her hospital bed. She was losing weight fast, though she did not know it. Me and Mom would visit and, like the colorectal surgeon, became genuinely concerned about her condition and the drastic weight loss. Jan could see the concern on our faces and one day asked for a mirror. We were hesitant for fear of her reaction of seeing herself.

Her cheeks were sunken in, her skin was dry and ashy. Believe me, you do not want to hear about how her hair looked under her scarf! Anyway, we gave in and gave her a mirror. The tears came streaming down her face as she looked horrified as she saw herself in the mirror. We consoled her, ensuring her that her weight loss and what she was going through was only temporary. Temporary for her meant six long months of being on a feeding tube and wearing an ostomy bag.

The colorectal surgeon, still concerned about Jan, sent her home to New Jersey with the equipment she needed. A nurse visited Jan regularly and I visited her as much as I could. After six long months, Jan was off the feeding tube and slowly gaining her strength. The recovery period took one year before Jan felt strong enough to go back to work. It was a struggle, but she was determined to get her life back to normal, of course, giving God His due praises.

Lin, on the other hand, had to have a partial removal of her large intestine, called a partial colectomy. With this procedure, the diseased portion of the colon is removed, and the cut ends of the colon are reattached, allowing waste elimination to perform normally. Lin's surgery was one month after Jan had surgery and for the most part, it went smoothly. She did not have any major complications other than the normal side effects like not being able to eat for a few months, feeling weak and whatever she ate was eliminated within minutes after digestion. Imodium A-D (an anti-diarrhea liquid that help decrease bowel movements) became her best friend. Lin lived in North Carolina and had her two daughters to give her support, but Jan and I were there in spirit and called daily to check in on her. The three of us were on the mend.

As for my brother Stan, well, he did not want any part of this madness! His visits with us became infrequent. I think it is a man's thing, not wanting to deal with doctors. Seeing his sisters suffer had to be difficult for him. And so, a year had gone by, and all was well, or so I thought. It seemed we just could not get a break.

***

In October 2002, the colorectal surgeon contacted me to remind me that he still needed to remove the remaining portion of my large intestine. It was something that had to be done; there was no doubt about it, just when things were going so well with me. Though I continued getting checkups by my chemotherapy doctor, I was going to continue furthering my education. I was feeling grateful to be able to share my testimony, and to be with my loving husband, with my family more (if that is even possible), teaching the children at church, and in charge of the junior ushers; things were going well. I loved what I was doing. I felt as though each time I decided to register for a college course or make progress, Satan would come and rear his evil head.

Yes, I knew, eventually, surgery was coming, but I hid the thought in the back of my mind. Now, it confronted me again, another colectomy surgery set for November. This time, Wesley, my family and I were more prepared. Since half of the colon was previously removed, by removing the remaining portion, the surgeon was able to reconnect a piece of my small intestine to the rectum, avoiding the need for an ostomy bag. I felt blessed that I did not have to wear an ostomy bag. I would have been devastated had I did.

I handled this as another test of my faith. This, too, was part of God's plan. This is what I had to persevere through, and it would only make me stronger in my faith and trust in God. Mom was with me and encouraged me along this bumpy journey. I had no idea why or what the Lord had in store for me, but it had to be something big! After all, I did not ask God to examine my heart and mind to confirm that I was truly a believer. No, I was not like David. **"Examine me, O LORD, and prove me; try my reins and my heart" (Psalm 26:2).** Nope, I did not feel that I needed another test to prove my faith in Him.

God knows everything! He is omniscient. He knows our level of faith and does not need to prove anything to Himself. The test is a trial to prove to ourselves the faith that we have in Him. We need to really know that our faith is real and what better way to find that out? The answer is through trials and tribulation — tests. When we go through a test, our faith develops perseverance and our walk with God matures. While we are going through a test, it is important to remember that everything works together for the good to those who love the Lord. **"And we know that all things work together for good to them that love God, to them who are the called according to his purpose" (Romans 8:28).** Those who do not know the Lord would fail the test, and/or simply give up or give in. It is better to view our tests as a blessing, and after the test is over, we can say: I have "stood the test." We tend to believe what we want to believe. And we intend to hear what we expect to hear. **"Then touched he their eyes, saying, According to your faith be it unto you" (Matthew 9:29).**

When you overcome challenges, it feels great! You are motivated and stimulated to push or press on to exciting things. It can be both uplifting and exhilarating. Acknowledging who is head of your life, and understanding why we as Christians are spiritually tested, empowers us to endure and take on challenges in a positive manner. Knowing that joy comes in the morning, and you have stood the test, you feel victorious.

When I awoke from surgery, there sat Mom. She was right there where I needed her. Of course, hubby was there, too. But having Mom there was the strong support that I needed. I was so happy to see her. She was a source of strength for me. There is nobody like a loving, supportive mother. After a few hours, it was time for hubby to go home and rest and get ready for his next day of work. Mom, of course, stayed with her "baby" girl.

Two weeks at home recovering, Mom, again, was right there taking care of her "baby" girl. She did her best to get me to eat, forcing me to eat applesauce, broth, vanilla pudding and drink plenty of liquids. I tried letting her know that I did not feel well, but she was persistent and did not want to listen to me. I tried my best to eat but just could not. I felt sick. Something was not right. I began to get sick, and Mom had to quickly run and get a bucket. Yes, something was wrong.

We contacted the surgeon and he asked, "What color is the vomit?" The vomit was green as in 'bile.' At this moment, I thought, "Can a girl get a break?" I was so outdone by all this drama, and of the different procedures I had already gone through. But I tried to hang in there and remember, God does not put more on you than you can bear. I continued vomiting in the bucket Mom gave me. I simply looked at my hubby and shook my head as if to say, "Oh well, it is what it is." I could see he was sympathetic and felt helpless as there was nothing he could do for me but comfort me, which is what I needed. We took Mom home and headed to the hospital emergency. I wept the entire way, holding my bucket tightly.

We arrived at the emergency room and got registered. Finally, when my name was called, Wesley and I were ushered to a semi-secluded room. You know what these rooms look like if you ever had to be taken to a hospital. The attending physician asked me, "Why the bucket?" He soon found out for himself as I had yet another round of regurgitation. I felt miserable, weak and terribly upset. I cried uncontrollably. I cried even harder when the attending physician informed me that he had to put a large tube through my nostril down to my stomach. He sprayed the tube, saying it would aid the tube to go down; it did not help! It was awful!

I was admitted and assigned to my hospital room, where eventually the colorectal surgeon was waiting. He said, "What took you so long? I've been waiting for you." I wanted to tell him to check with how slow the registration process worked, but I did not. X-rays and bloodwork were taken. It turned out that I had an infection and was put on antibiotics administered intravenously and other types of medications.

The next day, Mom came to visit me. We talked a little and watched the Winter Olympics on TV. I soon dozed off to sleep while Mom sat in a green colored chair in the corner across from the TV. I do not know how long I was asleep. When I awoke, I looked over at the television and could see that the Olympic skiers were competing. Then I called out to Mom. She did not respond. This was very strange, and I wondered why she could not hear me calling her. After all, she was awake. I looked down at my arms and tried to move. I couldn't move my arms! Panic set in as it appeared that I may be paralyzed. I called out to Mom again, still no response. Time passed. After what seemed like hours, finally Mom heard me calling her. I told her what I experienced, and we both concluded that I had an out-of-body experience, or had a hallucination. I never want to experience that again as it was scary. Probably, my taking various medications caused this reaction. Eventually, the regurgitation ceased.

After several days in the hospital, I was glad when the colorectal surgeon informed me that I was being released. My family was elated, and Mom felt so grateful that she commented that she would love to work at the hospital. I can only assume she felt as though she wanted to show her gratitude and appreciation, or give back to the nurses and doctors. Wesley was smiling like a Cheshire cat. He was so happy I was coming home. We had so much to be thankful for.

It felt great to be in my own bed, recuperating and knowing that God had done it again! Like Mom, I felt grateful and blessed. The recuperation period was hard and painful, as one can imagine. Having a surgical cut from just below your cleavage down past your navel meant that stomach muscles had been severed. And to think this was the second time. Thank God the colorectal surgeon was able to follow the path from the original cut. The incision did not look too bad, only that my navel is no longer in the middle of my stomach, rather more to the right side. It is not too odd looking though. Just know, I will never wear a bikini!

To have overcome yet another test allowed my faith to be more rooted and grounded. The more roots that are in the ground, the more support a tree has. "Deep roots will give us a strong foundation to withstand the elements, the trials, and challenges of life." It was clear to me that I had a testimony to share to those who needed it. Remember, I am somewhat of an introvert, and normally keep to myself. However, when I returned to work, there were those who were simply inquisitive regarding my hospitalizations, and those who really needed to be inspired, or needed to hear what the Lord had done for me. Some needed to hear of today's miracle and not only miracles told in the Bible; at least, this is how I felt.

The Lord empowered me to share my testimony to those who needed it. How do I know? Having had two colon surgeries and one rectal surgery and chemotherapy, I felt I was chosen to go through and now tell of God's wondrous works. I thank the Lord for His Grace and Mercy. Yes, I must tell it! **"But ye are a chosen generation, a royal priesthood, an holy nation, a peculiar people; that ye should shew forth the praises of him who hath called you out of darkness into his marvellous light; Which in time past were not a people, but are now the people of God: which had not obtained mercy, but now have obtained mercy"** **(I Peter 2:9-10).**

I was led to give a few co-workers my testimony; the response was moving. Some of us cried together, and some began to open up and release what they were going through. We all supported one another. It also made me feel relieved and amazed to know that I was not alone, and there were people who really care. Most of all, I needed to give my testimony, and by doing so, my testimony helped me recover. My release felt like a load of bricks fell off my shoulders. Perhaps, when in despair, or in difficult situations, I was focused on the situation, and therefore could not really appreciate nor rejoice for the blessing in the suffering.

"By whom also we have access by faith into this grace wherein we stand, and rejoice in hope of the glory of God. And not only so, but we glory in tribulations also: knowing that tribulation worketh patience; And patience, experience; and experience, hope: And hope maketh not ashamed; because the love of God is shed abroad in our hearts by the Holy Ghost which is given unto us" (Romans 5:2-5).

Also, during my suffering, there was no thought given that this suffering can't be "compared to the glory that he will reveal to us later." **"For I reckon that the sufferings of this present time are not worthy to be compared with the glory which shall be revealed in us" (Romans 8:18).** Having hope does not disappoint us. Now that I am out of "It," I look back and see where God brought me from. Praise God for the suffering and healing!

CHAPTER 6

Fire in the House!

Now that I have completely healed, things were looking better. Returning to work was therapeutic for me and I loved it and the people I worked with. Working was challenging, to say the least, because my job had become more intensified and required extensive travel abroad. As I mentioned before, flying was not my forte. Travelling with my manager, who is my friend, made flying somewhat comfortable. Having a close friend to converse with helped ease the tension and stress of flying. We travelled to Brazil (Sao Paulo), Spain (Barcelona), China (Shanghai), France (Paris) and several trips to other parts of Europe (The Netherlands, Ghent, Belgium, Amsterdam, Brussels). Each individual trip was for three weeks. Though these were business trips (we worked long hours and were on-call during the weekends), we were fortunate enough to have some leisure time to tour cities while in these countries.

China, Brazil, and Spain were my most enjoyable trips. It was in these countries where I did the most shopping and took many tours and beautiful pictures. Not that the other countries did not have beautiful sights, but I did not get enough time to shop like I wanted to. We also travelled regularly to Midland and Saginaw, Michigan on the company's private plane for business trips, though flying still was not one of my favorite things to do. Being away from my family three weeks at a time was difficult, and I longed to be with them during each trip. After long and tiring workdays, phone calls to home were made. Our conversations always started off with, "I miss you," and ended with, "Love you."

One clear, sunshiny day, in the month of September 2010, while on a business trip, I had my hubby on my mind, so I made a call home. The phone rang and rang. No one picked up the phone. So, I dialed again, knowing that Wesley should be home because it was his day off from work. Again, I dialed home but to no avail. I thought it was strange, but I figured perhaps he was in the shower. But then again, it was too early for him to be up and about at 7am. I continued to prepare myself for work. I had to be ready by a certain time, because we had to take the hotel shuttle bus to work. Once I was dressed and mentally ready for work, my hotel phone rang. It was Wesley. Instantly, I could tell that something was wrong. I heard it in his voice.

Wesley failed at trying to sound as if nothing was wrong. Immediately I was able to detect there was something amiss. I asked, "Honey, what's going on?" I can only assume that he did not know how to tell me there was an emergency that had occurred, and he struggled with how to explain what happened. His reply simply was, "Well, we have a serious problem at home." As you can imagine, panic instantly set in. A sudden wave of fear overcame me. My heart was pounding, and I had difficulty breathing. I felt like I was going crazy. If I could jump through the phone lines, I think I would have, if he did not quickly tell me what was going on.

After what seemed like hours, Wesley finally informed me that we had had a house fire. What? I felt dizzy and stunned; I had to sit on the edge of my bed before my knees gave out on me. I could not believe what I just heard. *How could that have happened?* was my first thought. However, what came out of my mouth was concern about the safety of everyone. I needed to know that he, my son, and the firefighters were safe. Wesley tried to calm me down, which I did, relieved that no one got hurt. Glory be to God. Neither Stephen nor Wesley were home at the time the fire started. He began to tell me that the fire was not too significant. Also, the fire started in our son's bedroom and was under investigation.

Of course, being worried, I was ready to go home. I told Wesley of my intent to contact the airport to change my plane ticket to an earlier departure date. My job was the furthest thing from my mind. They would certainly understand. The important thing was to get home to my family and not necessarily to see the damage. However, Wesley insisted that I not come home. He assured me that he, Stephen, and Jan would handle everything. I said, "Fine," and then we completed our call.

Leaving my hotel room with an uneasy feeling, I headed out for work. As I walked down the corridor, my mind went through the narrative of what occurred. I needed more assurance that the fire was not that serious. While waiting at the pick-up stop for the shuttle bus, I decided to call Jan on my cell phone. I knew she would be completely open; it was not that I did not trust what Wesley said, but like I mentioned before, I needed reassurance.

Jan answered her phone on the second ring, and I bombarded her with questions. One thing she informed me of really struck a nerve. A neighbor had published his video of our house fire on social media, which prompted my aunt, who lives in Wisconsin, to contact a family member! It was also on the local news network. Naturally, when I heard this, it made me upset and concerned about damages done by the fire. Obviously, if the news network thought the fire was newsworthy, the fire must have caused extensive damages.

Wesley and I recently had hardwood flooring installed in our kitchen and a new roof. We also had our basement finished a year prior to the fire. Our friends would always comment on the décor of our living room and dining room. It was all nice, but also only material things. Life was more important, but still I wanted to know what to expect when I returned home. Jan informed me that, unfortunately, the kitchen floor had to come up due to water damage. The firefighters had to make a huge hole in the roof, which is protocol. All our furniture had water and smoke damage, and of course, Stephen's bedroom was destroyed. The fire was contained to Stephen's bedroom and the attic portion that was just above his room.

Since the entire house was damaged by smoke and or water, every piece of furniture had to be replaced and the rooms had to be restored. The basement ceiling and walls had to be restored, and the furnace had to be replaced due to water damage; however, the floor tiles remained intact. The basement had not yet been completely furnished, and the few pieces that were there were salvageable.

Jan packed all my personal belongings and jewelry before the insurance agent arrived. She did inform the agent that my personal items had been taken care of. Wesley and Stephen picked through whatever they could salvage. The agent, I was told, took pictures of every item from the kitchen up to the attic. I was told she was a bit overwhelmed with all the clothing I had, and pots and pans we had! Wesley loved to cook, which is why we had so many. For me, there was no excuse for all the clothes I had; perhaps you could call me a miser or pack rat. Probably, there are others like me that have favorite clothing items that you find difficult to let go even if you can no longer fit in them! You have the mindset that one day, you will lose weight to fit into those items — though that day never comes.

Finally, it was time for me to travel back home from my business trip. As my manager and I sat on the plane, she could feel my tension and knew I was nervous about seeing my house. Together, we prayed that the Lord remove my fears and give me the strength needed to face what lay ahead. The flight was bumpy as the weather was cloudy with a slight chance of precipitation. Little conversation was said between us, and about twenty minutes into the flight, I simply closed my eyes and began to pray again, this time silently. Taking advantage of the lack of conversation, my manager pulled out her laptop and began to work. She knew I needed time to meditate. I was grateful for the quiet time.

Landing safely, it began to rain — not a heavy rain, but more of a fine, misty rain. The misty rain reminded me of the dream that my girlfriend interpreted for me. Just prior to getting off the plane, standing at the top of the stairs, I took a deep breath as if I would soon be approaching something horrible. I was preparing myself for what lay ahead. Home was only a few miles from the airport. Once we were off the plane, we gathered our luggage and hugged each other. Her hug was tight, and I knew she really was saying, "Hang in there, girly," which is what she normally would say when things got rough. Wesley drove up and greeted the two of us, and we departed the private airport.

Once Wesley and I were in the car, we hugged and kissed and spoke about nothing important — just small talk. We both were nervous; he was for me as he did not know how I would react when I saw the house, and me afraid of what I would see.

When we arrived at the house, he parked the car and I got out and waited for him. Looking up at the house, I thought, well, it doesn't look like we had a fire, at least, not from the view of the front of the house. As we walked up the walkway, I could see some items sprawled on our back lawn. On the second floor, the side bedroom window of Stephen's room was blackened, and the window was boarded. Wesley opened the front door, and instantly there was the charred or burnt odor from the fire.

The front porch and living room furniture were laden with soot. The dining room furniture was obviously water damaged and the tabletop cover had buckled; I thought the table survived, but when I lifted the tabletop, it had not. The dining room walls were completely covered with soot. I began to feel dizzy; but, I continued to analyze the damage. Hubby was holding my hand the entire time. We approached the kitchen. I gasped at seeing our beautiful kitchen floor. From the water, the flooring had begun to buckle. It was totally damaged, unsalvageable. I knew it would be hard to replace the flooring with the same color because it took us hours to find that color.

As we entered each room, Wesley reassured me that everything would be all right. I knew it would be all right because God had a purpose in all this madness! We were going to come out of this, too, but with stronger faith. We continued up the stairs to the bathroom and bedrooms. Stephen's bedroom was indescribable. It was too much for me! My immediate thought was, what if? What if my son had been asleep when the fire broke out? Awful thoughts began to flood my mind. It was time for me to get out of the house. Seeing our house in that condition was overbearing! The tears rolled down my face; I couldn't speak. It felt as if I had a lump or knot in my throat. It could not have been easy for Wesley, Stephen, or Jan to see our house like that, either. Thank God for the strength they had to be able to work with the insurance agent and the house restoration team.

Nationwide Insurance was on our side, as their slogan says. We were over insured, thanks to my wonderful husband's way of thinking of purchasing the best insurances and warranties we could afford. As for me, I am a little on the frugal side — tight when it comes to spending money. Anyway, the insurance company put us in temporary housing at a nearby hotel that housed displaced families. It was a really nice hotel and came with maid service; we, of course, did our own cleaning, but tipped the cleaning woman regardless. About one week later, Nationwide informed us that we had the option to search for a house to hold us up for the months that it would take to restore or refurbish our home. Nationwide provided us with food and clothing allowances. However, clothing that could be salvaged was sent to a facility that specialized in cleaning smoke-damaged items. Wesley and Stephen were able to find a few pieces of articles worth saving. I had my luggage, so I did not need to pick through the smoke-smelling clothes.

Leaving Wesley and Stephen again to go on another business trip, I left feeling like I was deserting them. I did spend a week with them, and we all felt relieved to be together, if only for a week. We made plans to look for a temporary house not far from where we currently lived. During my breaks at work, I searched and called a few rental places, but found none that suited us. We eventually settled for moving into an apartment not far from our house. God is so good! We were close enough to check on the progress that the restoration company made without traveling too far. In my absence, Wesley became friends with the manager and supervisor of the restoration company. This indeed was a blessing, because it gave Wesley some relief to be able to talk with people who had experience with house fire victims. They were able to encourage him and provide him with details on the process of restoring the house.

During this process, Wesley had taken a few weeks off from work, which was much needed. Upon my return, Wesley and I were puzzled and wondered what possibly could have started the fire. We live in a small community, so it was not unusual to see borough officers driving down your street. While leaving our house after one of our checkup visits, we stopped the fire chief, who happened to be driving by on that particular day. We questioned what the result was from the fire investigation. It was signed off as undetermined, though electric wires from my neighbor's house somehow ran up beside our wires in the back of the house — it seemed to be connected.

When I contacted the electric company, they were aware of the fire, and responded that they had everything under control, and we need not worry. They could not share any more information about the investigation. Well, that was fine with us, as long as we did not pay, or were not paying, extra electricity charges! To be clear, the house next door had been vacant for quite some time, and we recently got new neighbors. They are honest people and the wires had been there before they purchased the house. I believe both we and our neighbors were covered by God's protection, as the situation could have gone a completely different way.

Our testimony of how great God is, is that even though things seem their darkest, God shines a light on it. There is more to the saying, 'There is light at the end of the tunnel.' Though we may not see it, God has something for us (if you believe in Him). **"Light is sown for the righteous, and gladness for the upright in heart" (Psalm 97:11).** Understand that God's deliverance may happen or appear suddenly, yet it is sown and laid up in store for them. In other words, your deliverance, blessing, or miracle is just waiting to happen. Just hold on, help is on the way! **"And the light shineth in darkness; and the darkness comprehended it not" (John 1:5).** We, as a family, did not want to focus on the negative, but rather look past the disaster and be positive. We had to pick ourselves up and keep it moving! After all, God protected us from harm.

It took one year for our house to be replaced and for us to get our items returned from the cleaning restoration facility. All our items were individually tagged, making it easy for us to identify them when we were ready to pick up and bring our items home. It took us a month of driving back and forth from the restoration facility to retrieve everything that was stored. As for the house, it was stressful selecting flooring, color décor for each room, and furniture and appliances. In the end, the restoration of the house was simply beautiful. We were blessed to have an additional bedroom added which originally was part of the third-floor attic. We were able to install hardwood flooring throughout the first floor, including the kitchen and two bedrooms. We made the decision to have carpet only in the one smaller bedroom. What a blessing! God turned our trials and tribulations into triumph!

God can take something devastating and turn it into a blessing! Our ordeal again reminded me of Job (the Book of Job), though, thank God, we did not experience the death of anyone from the fire. We, indeed, were blessed. God blessed us, our lives and our home with His Spirit of love. For that we are thankful, because we realize how incredibly blessed we are to have each other and the love of God. And, we made new friends with the manager and supervisor of the restoration company. They both were the kindest and nicest people you could meet, especially under our circumstances. God put these people in our lives for a reason.

Now that we were settled in our 'new' home, and the house was fully furnished, we could finally give a sigh of relief. Truly, there is no place like home. We were happy, safe, comfortable, and feeling blessed. We returned to our normal routines. Wesley and I continued working, and Stephen was blessed with several promotions at his job. But, I felt that something was missing.

CHAPTER 7

Through the Storms

My brother, Stan, was always busy, but made time to visit the family. He affectionately called me "baby doll." Stan continued to be eager to challenge himself with new knowledge and skills. He attended many different seminars, and kept abreast on events held at his alma mater, the University of Pennsylvania. When I enrolled in the required math courses, I knew initially I would not have any difficulty passing. However, as I progressed to macro- and micro-economics, who did I reach out to? No one, but Stan! He came to my rescue, and I passed both courses with a "C"- Average. All my other courses I received "A's" or "B's," which is how I graduated "cum laude." Not only did he tutor me, but he also tutored one of my girlfriends (she is considered part of our family). Kudos to Stan for being such a great tutor! Stan was always looking out for his family.

One day, Stan stopped by our house to check up on how we were doing. As I opened the front door, I looked at him and could see that he looked very tired. He came in and sat down on the sofa. I sat in one of the chairs to the left of him. I immediately detected that he was in extremely poor health. There were bags under his eyes (worse than normal), his stomach was protruded and his legs were swollen. When I asked how he was doing, he simply made a comment like, "I'm hanging in there." He quickly changed the subject to me and Wesley.

In my heart, I knew he was extremely ill and most likely, colon cancer was the cause, along with his heart. I tried hard not to cry. It is awfully hard to see your loved one in pain when there is nothing you can do about it. I can't even begin to tell you how I felt not being able to help my brother through this illness. Knowing him so well, it was not a subject that he wanted to talk about.

I recall when I first informed my family that I had colorectal cancer; Stan was shocked. He said something to the fact that he had other issues to cope with. I thought, "What could be worse than what we all had?" The conversation went no further. I knew he had heart and back problems, but wasn't aware of any other health conditions he may have had. Back problems also run in our family, called spinal stenosis, which exists in our lower back. I don't know if this is hereditary but we siblings all have it.

Stan continued to attend seminars regardless of how he felt. One morning, he had car problems and asked me to drive him to one of the seminars being held at the university. I questioned how he would get home. He told me not to worry; he would get home the best way that he could. So, I dropped him off and continued my drive to work. Stan was retired and was determined to continue to live life to the fullest. He spent his time reaching out to help people, especially the elderly. Unbeknownst to us, he spent time visiting an elderly home and provided them with computer technical support. He loved working in electronics. He also kept busy as an R.O.T.C. (Reserve Officer Training Corps) instructor at a local high school in Philadelphia.

Stan was a retired Naval officer and loved teaching. As an R.O.T.C. instructor, the focus is to teach young men and women leadership skills, character development and make them aware of their responsibilities and privileges as Americans. He was so dedicated to the program that he would use his own money (really money he borrowed from his sisters) to take his 'kids,' the cadets, on field trips. He also saw to it that his nephew, Tyler, Jan's only child, learned archery. He would pick Tyler up every Monday after school to take him to archery lessons.

Heading to church on a beautiful Sunday morning, something told me to stop by Mom's. I rang the doorbell and proceeded to use my key to unlock the door. I always rang the doorbell prior to entering Mom's house; just a habit. As I reached the living room, an aunt, who lived with my mom, was sitting on the sofa to the left of Stan. Mom was sitting in her favorite reclining chair. When I looked at Stan, he looked very weak and held his head back with his eyes closed. He had his robe on. When he heard my voice, he opened his eyes and smiled. He then told me that he had a taste for cheesecake. I replied, saying, "Sure, I'll get you a cheesecake."

My aunt said, "What, you're going to get him a cheesecake now?"

I replied, "Yes, I would if the store was open. He's my brother and I will do anything for him." I told Stan that after church, the store would be open, and I would get him his cheesecake. I soon left and headed out to church.

During church service, my pastor asked if anyone needed prayer, and if so, to stand in the middle aisle. I quickly rose from my seat because I was going to stand in proxy for my brother. When my pastor asked what I wanted him to pray for, of course, I informed him that my brother was extremely ill. In my pastor's prayer, he said, "Lord, let thy will be done." I opened my eyes and looked at him. This was not the prayer I was expecting. I wanted him to pray for healing of my brother. I wanted my brother to live. The words I wanted to hear were, "In the name of Jesus, Lord heal her brother." I was devastated. I cried inwardly; my heart was heavy. Unlike when I was a child, I didn't make a promise to God that I would be the best Christian; instead, I went directly to a man of the cloth.

After church service, I stopped by Mom's to check on Stan. He no longer had the craving for that cheesecake. I felt awful and wished that I could have gotten it when he asked. Mom and my aunt looked at me with the most unforgettable expression. It was an expression of dire concern. Stan was not doing well at all. I realized then that Stan's health was quickly deteriorating. I went to my car and wept, then prayed, asking God to help him. When there is nothing left to do, all you can do is stand still and pray. At that time, I was not familiar with the scripture: **"Be careful for nothing; but in every thing by prayer and supplication with thanksgiving let your requests be made known unto God. And the peace of God, which passeth all understanding, shall keep your hearts and minds through Christ Jesus" (Phillipians 4:6-7).** I just knew I needed to pray for him.

The following morning, which was on Monday, January 9, 2011, Stan told Mom to call for an ambulance. I recall this date because it was the same day that a member of the United States House of Representatives was shot in the head. Afterwards, Mom phoned me, and my sister Jan; we met them at the hospital. My aunt remained at the house. Lin was living in North Carolina. We stood around my brother's hospital bed and watched the news regarding the U.S. House of Representatives. My brother was genuinely concerned about the shooting. All the while, I prayed inwardly that the Lord allow my brother to live. Our love as a family is a bond that is like heavy metal chain links — sturdy, and difficult to break.

When the doctors entered the hospital room, they informed us that they needed Stan's consent for emergency surgery. We encouraged him to sign the documents; he did. After what seemed like eternity, the doctors informed us that Stan's heart stopped just before the surgery, but he was resuscitated. The surgery could not be performed. We felt devastated at this turn of events. That meant they couldn't help my brother. I immediately ran to the ladies' room to cry and let out a scream. A young lady was standing by the sink washing her hands. I told her that my brother was dying. She told me not to give up, and that God has the last say.

On January 11, 2011, my brother got his wings. God took Stan. It was one of the worst days of our lives. A mother losing her only son and firstborn child. Sisters losing their only brother. A link in the metal chain had been broken. I researched on what a mother is called when she loses a child. What I found is that "there is no word for a parent that loses a child — because it never should happen." And as for siblings, it will be "lifelong upsurges of painful grief."

Much prayer is required by us and for us. He was so young, and Stan had so much to offer the young and old. We were looking forward to our first family trip; we had no specifics, we just knew this was something we had on the horizon. Spoiler alert — we can plan for events all we want, but God has the ultimate plan, and His plan will come to fruition. I'm not saying not to make plans, but the realization remains that tomorrow is not promised. It may seem harsh, but tomorrow may bring on evil things. **"Boast not thyself of to morrow; for thou knowest not what a day may bring forth" (Proverbs 27:1).** And, however, God has a plan for us to prosper and to not harm us. His plan is to give us hope, faith and a future. **"For I know the thoughts that I think toward you, saith the LORD, thoughts of peace, and not of evil, to give you an expected end" (Jeremiah 29:11).**

On the day of Stan's homegoing service, I arrived at Mom's where everyone agreed to meet for the limousine ride to the church. When I walked from the enclosed porch and into the living room, my heart skipped a beat. I thought that I was going to faint. Sitting on the sofa was my nephew, Stan's only child. Talk about having a twin. Oh, my goodness, he looked so much like Stan, and for a few seconds, I thought it was Stan. I burst into tears and my nephew, who was dressed in his Army captain uniform, simply smiled. He knew what I thought and responded, "Yeah, I know. I look just like my dad."

It was a very emotional homegoing service. Mom, my sisters, my husband, my brother-in-law and nieces were all touched by the attendance of the R.O.T.C. cadets (all in uniform), every armed force representative and the many distinguished guests, family, and friends. I found enough strength to give words on behalf of our family. I apologized for the long obituary, but I wanted to honor my brother by letting people know exactly what he accomplished in his short-lived years. Stan never bragged about his personal accomplishments, and some of what he accomplished, even we weren't made aware of.

In my encouraging words to the guests, I spoke about forgiveness — that people sometimes don't know why they're not talking to another relative; all they know is that an aunt, or a mom or someone didn't like so and so, therefore, neither do I. I also spoke about love, and encouraged the cadets to further their education; that is what Stan would expect them to do. He pushed for his students to learn self-esteem, to be educated and give back to the community. This was his legacy — an important part of his life!

After the service, I approached the cadets and thanked them all for attending. They informed me no thanks was needed because it was an honor, and it was the least they could do to honor a person they admired and respected. And that I should not worry about them because they all were headed for college! I hugged each of them, one by one. They touched my heart! My eyes welled up with tears.

Mom and my sisters could not talk; they were overwhelmed with grief, as was I. It was time to head to the burial site. It was a long, solemn drive. When we arrived at the cemetery, we were seated, and an officer had words and prayed. Next, the military gun salute, and chills ran down my body. A stillness of quiet surrounded us as we sat staring at the casket. More words of comfort and prayer, and we then instructed the military representative to present the neatly folded U.S. flag to Stan's son.

***

As if the death of our brother was not enough pain, two years later, we experienced yet another great loss. I received the call while I was at work, and I was completely speechless. All I could do was scream. My co-worker offered to drive me to my mother's house.

Jan had just recently talked to Mom, like she did every morning at 6am. Five minutes into their call, Mom told Jan that she would call her back. Jan responded saying, "But Mom, this is mother and daughter time." But Mom insisted on getting off the phone. Jan recalled that it was as if someone had walked into the house and required her immediate attention. Mom never returned Jan's phone call.

Ten minutes later, Jan described having a sharp pain in her stomach while she was getting her morning coffee at the kitchen area at her job. Jan then realized there was no return call from Mom. She proceeded to walk to her desk. She made the phone call to Mom — no answer. It was strange for Mom not to pick up. Jan had no choice but to call our aunt on her cell phone and instruct her to go downstairs to check on Mom. Mom was sitting in her chair, with her arms slightly raised, like she does when she is praising God. The phone was placed in the cradle, which Mom never made a habit to do. Mom could not be awakened. The paramedics were called, but it was too late. Mom had gotten her wings on November 12, 2013.

Mom's homegoing service (November 21, 2013) was to be the traditional African American Christian funeral, which was to not only mourn her death, but celebrate her life. My sisters and I were devastated and mourned her death, and did not feel the 'celebration of life' part. We were not yet at the acceptance stage of grief and, therefore, we did not feel joyous about celebrating when we no longer had a mother.

Though it is our belief that this loving woman of God departed us to go home to be with the Lord, it was painful. The service was touching. Two singers, one of whom was Mom's goddaughter, sang Mom's favorite song, "I Won't Complain." It touched us emotionally, because we did not tell them it was her favorite song, nor did we make any special song requests. Also, Mom's favorite scripture was read by my pastor, and it reads as such: **"If my people, which are called by my name, shall humble themselves, and pray, and seek my face, and turn from their wicked ways; then will I hear from heaven, and will forgive their sin, and will heal their land"** (2 Chronicles 7:14).

Days prior to the service, my pastor sat with us, and we talked extensively about Mom. My pastor listened to every word and story we shared with him about Mom. And by him taking the time to be with us, he delivered a heartfelt, personalized sermon. We were amazed and pleased on how he remembered so much that we shared with him.

For a moment, I forgot time as I sat looking at her lifeless body. My mind reflected on the wonderful mother and daughter times we had together. Oftentimes, Mom, Jan and I would go clothes shopping all day on Saturdays. Mom would select her dresses or suits and when it came time to pay at the cash register, Mom was nowhere to be found. Jan and I would just laugh. Mom knew her girls would take care of the bill. We girls would give and do anything for our mother.

Mom's death was totally unexpected. Though we know death is inevitable, there will always be an underlying fear that comes when you think or wonder who is next. Life is so unpredictable. The world we live in will bring many disappointments, sadness, fear and painful losses. But, when you have these ill-wanted feelings, it lets you know that you are alive. On the brighter side, we experience fulfillment, joy, happiness, love and peacefulness.

Feeling hopeless, shocked and numbed, we tried to understand why God allowed our mother to die suddenly. She was such an extraordinary mother. A mother's love "can never be compensated by anything else." There is no other love like the love from a mother; her love is unconditional. We are taught to see God in everything; but this was too much to bear. Yet, we continued to have trust and faith in God, knowing He would comfort us in times of sorrow.

Respecting my feelings, Wesley gave me my space on those tough days and believe me, there were many of those days. He was very much in tune to my grieving for both my brother and mother. He was aware and watched for the five stages of grief: denial, anger, bargaining, depression and acceptance, because he personally experienced it when his mother passed.

We didn't worry about the deaths of my brother and mother putting a strain on our marriage. Hard times strengthened our bond. Coping with the deaths of loved ones is difficult. Those who give support must be patient and realize there is no set timeframe for the grieving process to conclude. As time passed, there remained a sense of emptiness in my life. I was missing two people who I loved.

Being honest, with all the recent calamities, I couldn't help but have feelings of bitterness and anger. Against who, though? Certainly not against God. I felt as though my heart had broken into a million pieces. How was I ever going to overcome this loss? Now, having another link broken from the chain, there only remained us three girls. Life would never be the same. No father, no brother and now no mother. Why so much loss and pain? We loved our family so much. We sisters have a saying: "When we love, we love hard."

Like many people feel when they lose a loved one, death seemed unfair. Stan and Mom were compassionate, kind and loving people who gave so much to others, while people who are mean and go around hurting others are still here and live a long life. It just seems so unfair. When I mention how I feel, people respond saying, "God is giving those people time to get right." Well, saying it does not make me feel any better. Sorry if I seem cold. I'm just being honest. I miss my brother and mother so much!

It takes time for a broken heart to mend. Everyone reacts to death differently. It is important to find practical things to heal the hurt from a death. Oftentimes, I hold conversations with strangers, only if they appear approachable. Don't misunderstand me; it's not that I simply walk up to them and begin talking. I use rather a subtle approach. We first talk about the weather or something that occurred in the news, and depending on how I feel, I will share my feelings. It seems to help me when I talk to strangers, because I am more likely to get an objective point of view from them. There are people who understand that when you have tough days, you simply need to verbalize it or simply vent.

CHAPTER 8

The Battle to Survive

As the months passed, it became time for annual check-ups for my sisters and myself. Recall that we have familial polyposis, which caused each of us to have our colon removed. Now, it was time to have two procedures: 1) flexible sigmoidoscopy, which is a screening test for colorectal cancer and 2) an endoscopy, which is done to collect tissues for cancer of the digestive system.

Jan had her procedures performed first, then Lin had the procedures performed. The endoscopy results for both of my sisters concluded that they required the Whipple surgery! The Whipple procedure, also known as pancreaticoduodenectomy, is very risky and demands the precision of a highly specialized and experienced surgeon — we only found two specialists in our area. It usually is a procedure done on patients with pancreatic cancer. For my sisters, it was to prevent the cancer of the tumors or polyps that were found—a lifesaving surgery! The Whipple procedure is the removal of the "head of the pancreas, the first part of the small intestine (duodenum), the gallbladder and bile duct." All we could think is that our heredity problem was trying to kill us. Unfortunately, with this type of surgery, it came with many complications and changes to one's diet afterwards.

After Jan's surgery, her recovery did not go without issues. While visiting Jan recuperating at home, she went to the bathroom and within minutes her friend and I heard her screaming and crying. *Oh Lord, what on Earth could be happening*? I thought. I ran in the bathroom and there she was looking down at her belly. Her stitches had burst open at the seams! We literally could see the stitches undo one by one. I immediately ran to the house phone to dial 911. My nerves got the best of me, and I dropped the house phone, and it fell apart.

Her friend gathered Jan up and we rushed to the car, then dialed her surgeon while enroute to the hospital emergency room. All the while, we had Jan cover and hold her belly as we did not want anything exposed. It was a nightmare! The gastrointestinal surgeon met us at the emergency room and Jan was immediately escorted to surgery.

We prayed but knew that the Lord was going to take care of her. God did not bring her this far to leave her! The Word of God assures us that **"Being confident of this very thing, that he which hath begun a good work in you will perform it until the day of Jesus Christ" (Phillipians 1:6).** This, we genuinely believed. We were not giving up. Her journey had only just begun. And just because we have afflictions and trials and tribulations in life causing us to become overwhelmed, it does not mean to give up. Giving up is easy, but to persevere and press on is to understand that this is or may be one of the greatest tests of faith. God has a purpose for her, and for us. After this nightmare, Jan's recovery period went accordingly.

Next, Lin had her Whipple surgery scheduled. By this time, Lin had moved back here from North Carolina. We were thankful that she did because we certainly did not want her to have this type of surgery in North Carolina. Honestly, we did not think doctors there were as specialized as those here in the northeast (sorry North Carolina doctors).

Naturally, after what we went through with Jan, we were apprehensive. We prayed and prayed. We could not help but wonder why this was happening to us. After all, we were nice girls. People loved us. Our church friends called us the Morgan Girls and they knew if they needed something, we would be there to support them. The Morgan Girls were dependable.

Dependable or not, being Christians, we knew that God had a purpose for us. We thank God for making us aware of this hereditary disease and providing us with specialists in the field to be able to correct the dysfunctionality of our genetic design. With every human body, I believe there is imperfection; some are dormant, while others become life-threatening. This may sound a bit harsh, but it is what I believe. Accepting Jesus as your personal savior will help you endure or accept whatever plan that God has for you. I wondered what plan God had for me as my sisters underwent their Whipple surgeries.

Now that my sisters were recovering smoothly from their surgeries, it was my turn to get my flexible sigmoidoscopy and endoscopy procedures. Jan and I had the same physicians, so when I went for my procedures, the physician was knowledgeable of my history. The flexible sigmoidoscopy results were clear; however, the endoscopy resulted in my having to also have the Whipple surgery! Yes, undeniably, we were truly sisters! Was I upset? Of course I was. Unbelievable! Would I ever get a break?

You may have been in a situation where you knew something physically was not functioning correctly in your body but were afraid to address it. Then finally, when you decide to take control of your fear, you become somewhat relieved when you receive your diagnosis and understand the recovery period (hopefully a positive outcome). Personally, though it took me some time, with each medical diagnosis, I viewed them as another journey and accepted the fact that there would be plenty of ups and downs. The ups and downs just came with the territory.

Acceptance and knowing God is a protector was the only way to help me remain sane and deal with challenging situations. Being a Christian gave me that strength to continue to push through the difficult times and to call on the Name of Jesus to rebuke the power of Satan. Yep, Satan does have power, but God's power is omniscient and omnipresent.

The Scriptures tell us that Satan has power, but only if we allow him to tempt us with things we desire that may not be Godly. Satan is not a mind-reader. He is crafty and slick, like a snake, and can see what we find tempting, and he can hear our conversations and use what we say against us. The devil is walking around, seeking to see who he can devour. The written word says: **"Be sober, be vigilant; because your adversary the devil, as a roaring lion, walketh about, seeking whom he may devour: Whom resist stedfast in the faith, knowing that the same afflictions are accomplished in your brethren that are in the world" (1 Peter 5:8-9).**

My mother used to tell us, "Think all you want, but say not all you think." Her purpose in telling us was so that we would not say hurtful things to people. My take on it is, to be careful what you say because Satan is not omniscient, but he is listening. God already knows what we are thinking and what is in our heart, and God hears our prayers. With God, you don't have to say it out loud; He knows our thoughts.

Somehow after receiving my diagnosis, I sat there frozen as if I were cemented to the chair. I managed not to cry, but rather pulled myself together and accepted the next steps. An appointment had to be scheduled to get the full details on what lay ahead. This time, when I went to my appointment, Jan went with me. I told Wesley I would be fine having my sister with me. I felt he had been through so much with me that I'd give him a reprieve, since we were somewhat familiar with the procedure. My appointment with the same gastrointestinal surgeon as Jan was basically just formality; I knew what to expect. My surgery date was set for December 10, 2014.

Having a few months to prepare for my surgery, not without difficulty, my decision was to enjoy life and not allow fear to overcome me. My thinking was that the best thing was to trust the process that God laid before me. Collectively, we made plans that after the surgery, the family, those who wanted to, would go on a cruise. Relaxation and fun were what we all needed. I filled my mind with positive thoughts and thought about that cruise trip. Boy, I just couldn't wait! But for now, I had to settle with focusing on my work to keep my mind occupied.

One day, while at work, my manager and I were discussing a project and then our conversation turned to me. Remember, my manager and I were close friends, and she knew me well, and vice versa. I shared with her that I did not feel comfortable about having the surgery for some strange reason. She did not say a word. She just listened intently. I told her that I accepted the fact that it had to be done, but I felt different than when I was scheduled for my previous surgeries. I really could not explain my feelings; it wasn't fear. She said, "Let's pray about it." And we did, right there in her office. I put my apprehensions aside and got on with what I had to do. This occurred around mid-September.

Jan's birthday and mine are close together, so we decided this year to have a quiet celebration at home. This was right up Wesley's alley because he loved to entertain. To keep the celebration at a minimum, only family members were invited. There was lots of laughing and eating. Wesley prepared most of the food, which consisted of seafood salad, spare ribs, fried chicken, baked macaroni and cheese, and string beans. For dessert, Wesley purchased a birthday cake and vanilla ice cream.

Wesley would periodically look over at me when he didn't think I noticed. It was his way of checking on me to see whether I was enjoying myself. They sang happy birthday to me and then I made my wish and blew out the candles. Of course, no one knew that my 'wish' was really a short prayer asking God to have mercy on me and to allow me to live through the upcoming surgery. During the entire celebration, I tried hard to push the thought of the surgery out of my mind. I tried to focus on the conversations and join in by making brief comments, but nothing seemed to help. Everyone knew that, behind my smile, was concern about the upcoming surgery. Finally, the celebration ended, and everyone went to their respective homes. Exhaustion overcame me and I went to bed, leaving Wesley the task of cleaning up the remnants of the celebration.

The next morning, I apologized to Wesley for leaving him the task of cleaning. Of course, he understood the enormous strain I was under. The following weeks went too fast. Before I knew it, my day had come.

The day of surgery was somber. Nervous but calm, we walked to the registration desk. Once I was admitted and assigned to a temporary room in preparation for the operation, the atmosphere became uplifting. Jan, Stephen, and Wesley gathered around me and said a prayer for a quick recovery. It was touching, and I was pleased to be surrounded with love. Jan made all the necessary phone calls to our prayer warriors as the nurses began to prep me for surgery. If you've ever been in a Holy Ghost-filled Christian church, then you know about prayer warriors. For those of you who are unfamiliar with the term, a prayer warrior is "one who is connected to God intimately and consistently seeks to learn more about Him from His word, and uses their prayer time as a battleground for change." They are people who you know can get a prayer through to God or intercede for you.

My gastrointestinal surgeon entered the room and asked if I was ready. My response was, "Are you ready? Because all I have to do is sleep once the anesthesia is administered." Of course, he was ready, and with that, my family was escorted to the waiting area while I was being rolled down the long, cold corridor to the operating room. Although my mind was racing a million miles a minute, I was able to calm down and mentally recite The Lord's Prayer.

I was rolled into the cold operating room with a huge overhead lamp light that could probably spot the tiniest object on your body. There were several nurses and the anesthesiologist in the room. I recall talking briefly with the gastrointestinal surgeon, and then he asked me to count backwards from the number twenty. I don't know if I ever reached number one; I was out for the count. It's important that I point out that Jan had a phone conversation with one of the administrative staff of my gastrointestinal surgeon prior to my surgery. The gastrointestinal surgeon was not available to take her call because he was on his way to somewhere upstate, I think to New York, to put down his dog that was ailing and old. She also said that he was visibly upset about his dog. My surgery was within a day or two of his return. I am not sure whether this had anything to do with what occurred later.

The surgery took six hours, which was longer than expected. This was due to the adhesions that had formed from my previous surgeries. According to the gastrointestinal surgeon, the adhesions were "hard as steel," which made them exceedingly difficult to sever. After the six hours of surgery, I was wheeled to a semi-private room where I was to recover for seven days. I do recall two things: 1) Hearing my nurse say, "Her work is never done," and 2) Me waking up and asking my roommate if I was to chew the ice cube the nurse had given me or suck on it. This point on is an account from what my loving sister Jan had informed me.

Jan sat with me for hours after the surgery and finally went home. The next morning, upon her arrival, my roommate informed her that she physically crawled out of her bed to seek a nurse for me because I was delirious. She said the nurse never came to see about me and that the nurse did not like her and therefore ignored her request. Jan thanked her kindly.

When Jan saw me, my body was soaked with perspiration, and I looked pale. Instantly, she ran to the nurse's station to have the gastrointestinal surgeon paged. Trust me, Jan was not meek and quiet about it. I know her. She let it be known that something awful was wrong with me and to get the surgeon immediately. Since she had the same surgery, she knew exactly how far I should have progressed. She may have used some choice words to the nurses; I didn't ask her. Thank God my surgeon arrived within minutes.

Indeed, my gastrointestinal surgeon agreed that something was terribly wrong. A CT (computerized tomography) scan was taken, which resulted in the need of emergency surgery due to a pancreatic leak. Phone calls were made to Wesley, who was at work, but they went unanswered, and someone with authority had to consent to emergency surgery. So, Jan was asked to consent. The doctor explained the complexity of the surgery and the decision was up to her. Either I lay there and die, or take a chance on another surgery. I cannot imagine the pressure that was put on her. With shaking hands, Jan signed the consent form. The surgery was immediately set and within an hour, I unknowingly was taken back into surgery. Phone calls were continually made to Wesley, but to no avail.

My sisters and I, as you can tell, are awfully close. God had Jan right where she needed to be. My sisters are truly a gift from God. We have a lifetime relationship. Of course, we do not see everything the same way, but the love we have will always remain. If it weren't for Jan, I would not have lived after the initial surgery.

And, by the way, about that nurse who said her work was never done and did not seem to want to care for me, she got removed from that floor. Jan's best friend's daughter was the head of the nursing staff at multiple hospitals. Once she got word, she had the nurse removed, and had me moved to a more caring unit on a different floor. One of my new nurses said, "You know people in high places." Little did he know that the one I know in a higher place is Jesus!

For whatever reason, I had developed a pancreatic anastomosis dehiscence and fistula formation following my Whipple procedure. This also caused a creation of a new anastomosis, and wide abdominal drainage, as well as ventilator-dependent respiratory failure, which led to the need of a tracheostomy. With this diagnosis, I was at death's doorstep. After the emergency surgery, I was taken to the Critical Intensive Care Unit (CICU), where several different machines were connected to me as my vital signs were dropping. I was also put on kidney dialysis, and a heart machine. Blood clots formed and an IVC filter had to be inserted via surgery by the interventional radiologist. All in all, one of my nurses informed me there were a total of seven machines connected to me at one time. I spent three weeks in the CICU.

After being in the CICU, they moved me to the Intensive Care Unit, and I remained there for an additional three weeks. Jan told me all my friends who visited me and prayed for me. I had no concept of time, nor who visited or didn't visit. There were many days where the doctors did not know whether I was going to live through this ordeal. Jan recalled the time when she and her son, Tyler, visited me, and she left Tyler with me as she went for coffee. The minute she stepped away, something with my trach happened, and blood went everywhere. Perhaps it was due to blood clots that had formed and forced their way out of the trach tube. Tyler moved quickly to get help. When Jan arrived, nurses and doctors surrounded my bed. Tyler was in shock and in tears. The situation scared him, and Jan consoled him and apologized for leaving him alone with me.

Of course, none of this was her fault. Was it anyone's fault for all that happened to me? Was my surgeon so emotional about his dog that he was not as fully focused during the surgery as he should have been? Believe me, we all had the same question. However, we had to get past the questions and reasons and focus on my recovery.

This ordeal was devastating to both my husband and family. I was kept heavily medicated and unable to communicate. Three months later, I opened my eyes and looked directly at the calendar while one of my nurses stood by, watching me intently. Mentally, I began to count the months from December 10, 2014, to present. I realized that I missed Christmas, New Year's Eve, Valentine's Day, and we were now at the end of March 2015! My nurse must have read my mind because she looked at me and she said, "Yes, you've been with us for three months."

I could not comprehend, or even think, what had happened to me. My mind was focused on my being in the hospital for three months. Though I did not talk, I hadn't realized that I had a trach. Within minutes of waking up, several doctors appeared at my bedside. The interventional radiologist informed me he wanted to remove the trach. Well, what could I say? I had no concept of what was going on. I simply laid there as he removed the trach. Unfortunately, it did not go well. My body was not yet ready for me to breathe on my own. I won't go into details on my reaction when he removed the trach. The bottom line is that the trach could not be removed yet; I had to deal with having it a little longer. There was much concern about the amount of time I had the trach and the other machines. From what I recall, the longer I was on the machines, the less chance I had of them being removed. Long-term use could cause permanent dependency.

My mind was not yet at the point where I could pray, think or make any decisions. I simply laid in the bed, not able to move. From being immobile for three months, the weight of my body felt like a ton. I could hardly move my arms or legs. When Jan arrived, all I could do was watch for her facial reactions to clue me in on just how bad my situation was. She cried, all the while rubbing my hand and assuring me everything was going to be fine. Wesley walked in shortly thereafter. My eyes welled up in tears. I could see the pain in his eyes; just to see me lay there, oblivious of the nature of my condition, was hard on him and everyone else.

My nights were filled with hallucinations or horrible dreams of my own funeral and visions of someone sitting beside my bed dressed in all black, just waiting. I am sure the medications I was on were causing my hallucinations. No matter how hard I tried to wake up, I couldn't. This was such an awful experience that I kept it to myself until now.

Jan kept close friends and family members abreast of my condition. She finally got ahold of a close friend of ours, a bishop, who had no idea of what was going on with me. Well, after Jan hung up the phone, she told me the bishop was on her way! The bishop visited me and prophesied that every machine was going to be removed. A few hours later, well before the bishop even got home, the machines were one by one removed. Look at how God worked! He places people in your life for a purpose. The bishop had been a close friend of our mom and now is part of our family.

My guess is that a few days later, the doctor of Interventional radiology visited me again. Jan was right there by my side, praying that this was the moment. It was time again to try to remove my trach. A few nurses came in, I guess to witness and provide support. Success! No negative response. A speech therapist was there and asked me to say a few words to ensure my vocal cords were not damaged. When I spoke, my first words were, "Thank you, Jesus." I can only assume that after having a trach, one would feel a knot every time you swallowed. It began to be annoying, but most importantly, I could talk.

The doctors had to insert a tube through my nostril down my throat, which I had to have for what seemed like forever. With the tube, I did not want to talk or swallow. It was so uncomfortable. I could feel the hardness of the plastic tube. It made me want to simply sleep the days by until they could remove it.

Once the tube was removed, thank God there was no damage, but later I would receive speech therapy along with physical therapy. The physical therapy was exceedingly difficult and tiring. Just think, if you hadn't used your muscles in three months, walking was almost impossible. Getting out of the bed was undoable without assistance from the nurse. The nurses and physical therapist were very encouraging and when my sisters, Wesley and Stephen came to visit, I would make it a point to get up and walk so they could see my improvement. Trust me, my walking was terribly slow and not without a walker. They showed exuberance over my small steps, but it was a huge victory.

The next accomplishment was walking up stairs. I remembered a commercial that would encourage a baby, saying repeatedly, "One foot in front of the other." I kept that saying in my head but changed it to, "One step at a time, nice and slow." Learning to climb the stairs was more challenging than learning to walk; it took more effort. The nurses encouraged me, and I encouraged and pushed myself. I wanted to go home.

As I mentioned before, God will use our tests to encourage others to seek Him. And there are times in our lives we find that we must encourage ourselves, rather than waiting on others to do it for us. Encouraging yourself is just as important as encouraging others. We all need that extra push or encouragement. We all, at some point, need to feel valued, and feel that what we do or accomplish matters. When we feel encouraged, it gives us the strength to do what we feel we can't do. It helps us hold on when we feel we can't hold on any longer. It gives us courage to try things we may not otherwise try. Encouragement makes you effective! The Word of God says: **"Wherefore comfort yourselves together, and edify one another, even as also ye do" (I Thessalonians 5:11).**

After each session, sleep became easier for me. After the exhausting therapy, I couldn't wait to get into the bed. At times, I disliked seeing my physical therapist, because I knew I would have a good workout but just didn't feel up to it. But the words "not today" were not an option. There was no "let up" from physical therapy. After weeks of physical therapy with a walker, I graduated to using a cane. It may sound like a small victory, but it was a huge victory for me. It was one step closer to being released from the hospital.

My days were filled with visits from multiple doctors explaining to me what had occurred, and what the next steps would be. Feeling stupefied, I just listened after trying to absorb everything I was told. The associate to my surgeon must have read my facial expression because one day she visited me and handed me a typed document on plain paper (no letterhead) which included everything that happened to me from the initial surgery, the emergency surgery and to the present. I thanked her graciously.

At the time, I still was not up to comprehending too much, but I knew it was important and I would want to read it at some point. When Jan and Lin came to visit me, I handed them the document. They were puzzled at why the document was not on official letterhead and it was not signed. Obviously, after reading it, it seemed the information provided may prove some negligence on the doctor's part. Believe me when I say, a lawsuit was the furthest thing from my mind. The important thing was for me to survive this ordeal and go home. What was done was done. I didn't lose a limb nor was I paralyzed. *I'm good*, was my thinking. I thank God for who He is and for bringing me through. I just wanted to give God the glory and not worry about bringing forth a case against a doctor. God guided the doctor's hands and gave them knowledge and the skill to perform such a difficult surgery, and for that I am thankful and grateful. After all, doctors are human, too, and can make mistakes, and in my case, I was alive and recovering. That's all that mattered to me. I did keep the document, as it was clear and precise about the medical procedures and what occurred.

Money is not all that important to me, but my soul is. As a songwriter wrote, "You can have all the riches and gold, but I would rather have Jesus." If you don't have good health, then wealth means nothing. You can have all the money you want, but it will go quickly. **"Wilt thou set thine eyes upon that which is not? for riches certainly make themselves wings; they fly away as an eagle toward heaven" (Proverbs 23:5).** There is an old gospel song entitled "I'll Take Jesus for Mine." The lyrics say something like this: "You can have this whole wide world but give me Jesus. I'll take Jesus for mine. You can have silver and gold and riches untold but give me Jesus. I'll take Jesus for mine." All I wanted was to live and be healthy.

As my recovery continued, my surgeon took a blood test to ensure my kidneys were functioning properly. My creatinine level was abnormally high, which presented a risk of death. Therefore, a visit to the interventional radiologist was necessary to have tubes inserted into each side of my belly, which extended to the outside of my body with a bag attached to my legs to collect the dark green fluid. If it wasn't so serious, you would have thought I looked like RoboCop, armed and ready for battle. Still, I remained prayerful and hopeful and encouraged myself that this too shall pass, remembering that God won't give you more than what you can handle. There was no choice for me but to hold on and hold out because something greater is coming! My family and friends continued to hold me up in prayer. The tubing remained attached for a few weeks as I progressed with strengthening my legs. Finally, a breakthrough—the tubing was being removed and I was prescribed creatinine shots every twelve hours. The time had come; I was being released from the hospital.

Again, thank God for my sisters, who took turns to stay with me and give me my shots at midnight and late mornings. They both set the alarm clock so as not to miss my dosage. Wesley was so appreciative for their help and thankful that he was able to get the proper rest he needed. Stephen was also appreciative and offered to help whenever he could, bringing me soup, though I was not able to hold down any liquids.

Wesley, my wise husband, contacted the doctor because one day, I began to get sick and very weak. Yep, you guessed it! Back to emergency room I went. These were trying times for me and at this point, I was going along with whatever I was told to do. A feeling of helplessness and depression took hold of me, but my support team was there and in action, encouraging, pushing, and reminding me that God had a plan, and that after this, I would have a great testimony. Truly, I do not know what I would have done without my support team.

Readmitted to the hospital again, due to fevers and persistent abdominal collections from a low-grade pancreatic anastomotic leak, I was started on IV octreotide to limit the pancreatic secretions and help with anastomotic healing. Interventional radiology drainage tubes had to be reinserted while under general anesthesia. Within one day of being in the hospital, I started feeling so much better. After three or four days, I was released from the hospital. However, the drainage tubes would remain, and I would be treated as an outpatient with ongoing visits with the gastrointestinal surgeon. There were no complaints from me. This was progress! The timeframe for having the IV drainage tubes was short and I was recovering at a good pace. Within two months, my strength had returned, my faith was even stronger and things were looking up. Being home helped speed up my recovery and I began to think about going back to work.

Once I was cleared by my doctors sometime in July 2015, I was excited to be able to, at first, work from home, then months later, physically go in to work and have some normalcy return to my life. My workload had picked up where I left off, and business travel to Michigan was soon again part of my work routine. My manager and I were scheduled to work in Michigan for two weeks. When we arrived in Michigan, my co-workers were elated about my return and the busyness hadn't changed. We worked long hours and took short lunch breaks.

By the second week, I woke up feeling great and put on a smidge of makeup. I was ready to take on whatever work issues we had to address that day. I would say around 11:00 am, a co-worker of mine looked at me and asked whether I was having any bowel movement issues. I was taken aback and asked her what made her ask such a question. Her response was because the color of my eyes was "yellowish," indicating bowel blockage. I calmly walked to the ladies' room and indeed, my eyes were a yellowish color. Well, I was alarmed! Indeed, this was an indication that I had jaundice, though I didn't know that at the time.

I returned to my work area and asked my manager to look at my eyes, and immediately the decision was made that I was going to Urgent Care, who in turn sent me to the local hospital emergency room. Sharing my medical history with the doctor, he knew there could be a serious problem. A CT scan was ordered. In viewing the scan, the doctor informed me that since my digestive system was so unusual (due to the removal of my colon and the Whipple procedure), he could not help me. I had to promise to get on the plane and immediately head to the hospital. The doctor informed me my CT scan record would be forwarded to my doctor, who would be waiting for me. I began to feel a little panicky, but thanks to my manager's support, she kept me calm. She adjusted my return flight ticket to leave that same day on the company's private plane. On the plane, sitting alone, I began to pray and wonder what the problem could be. I had already contacted Wesley to meet me when the plane landed. Wesley was off that day, which was such a relief.

When Wesley and I arrived at the hospital, we were instructed to go to the Interventional Radiology Unit. I thought this was strange, as we expected to visit with the surgeon. However, my surgeon had already scheduled me to have a small incision made to insert a tube in my belly that would go down toward my rectum. The tube would help widen the hole that was causing the bowel obstruction. The plan with the tubing was that every three months, I would need it changed to a different size — large, medium, then small. And with each change, general anesthesia would be administered. My instructions were to keep the tube clear via flushing. Flushing the tube which hung from my belly was simple and caused no pain. With the understanding that it would be nine months of me having the tube along with its bulkiness, a desperately needed vacation was in order.

With three months completed with the largest tube, I was unequivocally ready to go on our annual cruise. Even though it was the month of November 2015, and we never took vacation during the cold season, I was ready. Nothing would get in the way of a desperately needed vacation. So, the week of our birthdays (Jan and mine), which is in November, Wesley, Stephen and I, along with Jan, Tyler, a family friend and two other family members, decided to go on a cruise. It was well deserved by all, but was it the best vacation? Well, being that it was in November, the weather on the islands where we docked was not as warm as we had hoped. Jackets were required and there were hardly any vacationers on the islands. For whatever reason, the lack of the hustle and bustle of people seemed to damper the excitement of being on the islands.

Due to the cool weather, we only shopped and toured each island for a few hours and then headed back to the ship. I felt more comfortable and relaxed while lounging on our balcony, soaking up what little sun there was. Entertainment on the ship was awesome as usual and the specialty food served was delicious. The fact remained that being away from home and getting some rest and relaxation was just what we needed. No schedules, no doctors' appointments, no tests, no nothing; everyone was on their own to do whatever they wanted to do. And no, this was not the best vacation, but acceptable given my circumstances.

Our past cruises were always taken during the early summer months. For us, being able to sit out in the sun on our balconies or relax in the warm but comfortable jacuzzi with a cool soft drink was totally satisfying. There were multiple pools, which were crowded most of the time. Special pool side events were scheduled which could be hilarious. The participants, who were fellow cruisers, would have your stomach aching from laughing so hard. It shows there are people who will do almost anything to win a competition. The chance of cool days or rainy days were few and far between during the times we selected to cruise. This was very different than the November cruise, but we made the most of it, anyway.

Once our cruise was over, we quickly settled back into our normal routine of working and me helping administratively at my church. During the month of April 2016, after nine months of having the interventional radiology tube, it was finally time to have it permanently removed. **Hallelujah!** Thank you, Jesus, for freedom! Having to flush the tube daily and worrying whether it was doing its job, and the fact that people could see the bulge on my side, was always a concern and made me conscious of it. Only time would tell if the opening would remain opened and no longer cause me problems.

Time quickly passed, and my life was back to normal. Wesley, Stephen and I were enjoying life as a family. It seemed that there was more love, if that was possible, in our household. We would gather in the kitchen during dinnertime and sing, act silly and simply enjoy each other's company. My company allowed employees to work from home, which I eventually did, though at first it was not something I wanted to do. Working from home gave my body more time to heal, though work kept me busy and up at late hours of the night. All in all, the fact remained, we were blessed and happy about what God had done in our lives. God brought me from a mighty long way! We had so much to be thankful for.

We would take the time to consider how the Lord has walked with us and has been there for us, walking beside us through the storm, being faithful even though at times we ourselves fell short of His glory. God continues to protect us, and He has been good to us even in our shortcomings. Even in your personal situations, when you may have felt like giving up, God is there to deliver you from your imperfections. Even when we have done wrong, God is still calling us to come into the safety of His arms. He delivers us from the dangers, seen and unseen, miraculously giving us the victory through life's challenges. Things would be different had He not been faithful and good to us. Similarly, like David, we ought to be amazed at how the Lord takes good care of us. I suggest reading the following passage of King David's Prayer found in **1 Chronicles 17:16-27.** Below is a caption of verses **16-19**:

> **David's Prayer**
> **"And David the king came and sat before the LORD, and said, Who am I, O LORD God, and what is mine house, that thou hast brought me hitherto? And yet this was a small thing in thine eyes, O God; for thou hast also spoken of thy servant's house for a great while to come, and hast regarded me according to the estate of a man of high degree, O LORD God. What can David speak more to thee for the honour of thy servant? for thou knowest thy servant. O LORD, for thy servant's sake, and according to thine own heart, hast thou done all this greatness, in making known all these great things"** (1 Chronicles 17:16-19).

While we are amid our own personal storm or war — whether it be health issues, financial issues, mental issues, abusive or broken relationships — it behooves us to take stock in what the Lord has already done for us. Looking back on how we survived, and seeing how the Lord blessed us and our loved ones, serves as inspiration and encouragement to help us look forward to the next day. Unfortunately, sometimes, when we look back, we focus on the problems we encountered or what we lost, more so than on the blessing. No matter how small we think our blessings are, each blessing should be considered as significant. Our countless blessings solidify or confirm that God can and will do just what He said He would do. **"God is not a man, that He should lie; neither the son of man, that He should repent: hath he said, and shall he not do it? Or hath he spoken, and shall he not make it good" (Numbers 23:19).** Keep the faith that victory is on the horizon!

CHAPTER 9

Michael: A Need to Rebuild

Though I continued to be productive at my job, taking care of my responsibilities at home and handling the administration duties and events at church, I had a sense that there had to be more for me. There had to be something that could fill the emptiness. I had so much love to share and so much to offer; there had to be something or someone that I could help. That's when it hit me! Fostering a child would fulfill my emptiness. It would be a twofold solution. Providing love, security, safety and nurturing for a child in need would benefit our family, especially me.

It was a lot to ask of Wesley, but being the type of character he was (loving and giving), he agreed to become a foster parent. It's easy to say you want to become a foster parent, but there is a lot of work you must put in and lots of paperwork. It is a long approval process to go through. It is required to have a physical examination as proof that you are free of communicable diseases and that you are in good health. There are three clearance checks you need to pass: criminal history, child abuse and FBI. Qualifications for us personally were to provide a safe place, be humorous, fun, loving, flexible, caring and be financially stable. Three letters of references from associates (not family members) were required. We also had to provide our marriage license, proper homeowner's insurance and car insurance, driver's licenses and proof that we own our home. The paperwork included a biography from each of us, complete with a description form of the preference of race, age, and sex of the child we wanted, and other important information to help match us with a child. A form they provided had to be completed giving them our monthly budget, and a list of bank and investment information. We thought some of the required information was a bit too personal, but we thought it worthwhile, and the bottom line was that a child would have a good home.

The state where we live requires that you attend 6 hours of training sessions, attend one-hour monthly meetings and complete 20 hours of online courses in different areas, such as being aware of child abuse signs, knowledge of safety for children and identifying needs of children. Training hours are required on a monthly and yearly basis. As a foster family, a caseworker will be assigned to visit our home monthly to ensure things are going well. For our house to be qualified, it had to be inspected and equipped with a fire escape plan and be free from fire hazards. The water had to be set at a certain temperature and it had to be equipped with fire extinguishers.

Some of you may be wondering or questioning why it is necessary to provide financial information and why fostering was important to us, or if fostering children was worth all the investigation and information gathering? For Wesley and me, the reason for becoming foster parents was simple. Every child has the right to a kind, loving, safe and secure home. Children deserve and need stability and normalcy in their life. Not all, but some "children placed in foster care have been abused, abandoned or neglected. They need to be shown that there is hope for a better life." We not only could provide the basic needs, but we also would demonstrate good communication skills and knew how to be stern when necessary. Both Wesley and I use authoritative parenting styles, though at times we fit both authoritative and permissible styles. Basically, what I am saying is that there should be balance when raising children, and there are many good reasons why becoming a foster parent was a great decision for us.

Support from my siblings increased our decision to move forward with becoming foster parents. After attending our first training session, we learned that the birth mother is given help via training classes to overcome the situation that put her in danger of having her child taken temporarily or put in the situation for adoption. The birthing parent can also connect to the foster parent(s) who could be seen as a role model. This sounded to us like a win-win situation for all involved. Knowing that the goal of the social services agency we signed with is for reunification of parent(s) and child made us want to become partners of the organization. It seemed the organization had a genuine interest in the welfare of children and had respect and compassion towards the birthing parent.

We did give thought on the variety of emotions we would go through when the time came to give a child back to the birthing parent. However, our desire did not waver to become foster parents, because at the end of the day, it is the child's safety and welfare that is the priority. We would cope with the transition at that given time.

As time passed, we grew impatient while waiting for "our" child. We had completed the necessary courses, which included CPR safety training. Our house passed inspection and everyone in the house passed the background checks. We purchased furniture for the child. We were ready mentally and physically. I prayed, asking God to send us a child and let the child's parent(s) be as reasonable as one could be, given the fact that placing your child in foster care has to be a difficult thing to do. Coincidentally, it seemed every time I'd get into my blue Volkswagen Jetta and turn the radio on, an advertisement about becoming a foster parent would be on. And, also, I seemed to be more attentive to commercials on television that would be showing pictures of children in need of food, love, and security. I took the "repetitive messages" as an obvious way that God was getting our attention and confirming that fostering was definitely what He had planned for us.

We continued to work and carry out our normal routines. By this time, things were settling down, and I was less stressed and less depressed about the loss of my brother and mother. Keeping busy helped keep my sanity. Wesley and I would sit at the dinner table, talking about the usual topics, and then eventually the conversation would turn to fostering. And of course, the question of "When will we get 'our' child?" would come up. Of course, it was more me than Wesley who was growing impatient. Stephen would join in on the conversation and let us know whether he would prefer a boy or a girl. And we all agreed and that is what we informed the social services agency; a little boy would be a perfect fit in our family. So, we continued to wait months until finally we received a call from the social services agency.

It was on a Saturday morning in July 2016 when our phone rang. Unexpectedly, the voice on the other line was that of the social services agency caseworker. She began telling us that they had a two-year-old African American boy who needed to be placed. Excitedly, though holding back my joyfulness of hearing such fantastic news, we listened anxiously. My heart was beating fast. My eyes were wide as saucers, according to Wesley. I stood up pacing around our coffee table as we received detailed information about "our" child. Then the anticipated information was told to us — the arrival time. Yes! The caseworker was going to bring "our" child within two hours the same day we received the call!

The weather in July was hot and a little humid, but it was the best time for us to be placed with "our" child. Immediately, in my mind, I began planning our summer activities. Wesley was excited and nervous at the same time. He went upstairs to check the bedroom to ensure it was ready, which it was. After all, we had been preparing for this moment for quite some time. Wesley and I sat on the sofa, awaiting the arrival time, and talked about how "our" child might react when he meets us. We prayed that "our" child would not be afraid or cry after the caseworker, but we were ready for anything at this point.

Finally, the doorbell rang, and I of course ran to greet them. The handsomest little boy stood on our doorstep, looking up at me with the biggest smile on his face. I asked him for his name, and he replied, "Michael" (not his real name). I responded, "Well, come on in, Michael." I didn't introduce myself as I didn't know what to call myself. Saying, "I'm Ms. Juanita" sounded too formal, so I didn't say anything at the time. I escorted Michael and my caseworker into the living room where Wesley was standing by this time. Wesley introduced us by saying, "I'm Wesley and this is my wife, Juanita." Okay, thanks for formalities Wesley! Anyway, we all sat down and let the caseworker take the lead.

Obviously, the caseworker had already explained the situation to Michael because he seemed wonderfully comfortable and ready to show me his personal belongings. We all were elated to see how comfortable Michael already seemed. As Wesley and the caseworker reviewed some of the policies, Michael and I were having our own conversation. Michael was excited as he showed me the few toys he had brought along. Looking through his belongings, I could see that we would need to do more clothes shopping than what we already had done. Our caseworker previously informed us of Michael's size, but we didn't want to purchase too much without him being with us to ensure the items fit properly.

It wasn't long before it was time for the caseworker to leave, once she was sure that Michael felt comfortable and safe. Wesley and I stood to escort the caseworker out, and Michael grabbed my hand as we walked her to the door! WOW! It warmed my heart to feel his little hand in my hand, and so quickly to see that he felt comfortable with us. It was an amazing feeling. Wesley gazed at me, and I knew he too was thinking how blessed we were to have Michael, and that there were no negative vibes or crying from Michael. Michael was now a member of our family.

So, we celebrated by ordering pizza, which was one of Michael's favorite foods, according to the information we learned from his personal history. Once the pizza order arrived, we went to the kitchen and sat at the kitchen table. Wesley picked up Michael and sat him in the only swivel chair we had. The rest of us sat in the high bar chairs. Michael quickly noticed that his chair was different and asked why. We told him we thought he would be more comfortable in the swivel chair, but if he wanted, we could switch chairs. And that's exactly what he wanted, a chair like ours. Looking at this situation, it came to my attention that Michael did not want to be viewed as different or the outsider. And by having a different chair, he felt different. So, it seemed that we had a lot to learn about becoming parents again. Lesson number one—children do not like to be viewed as different or special. And a swivel chair for a young child is not safe.

As we began to get more comfortable while eating pizza, we noticed Michael's vocabulary. He was above average for his age, in my opinion. He used words like "actually," "probably," and "maybe," and questioned what was on the pizza, and what were we going to have for dinner. I responded by saying one pizza had pepperoni on it and that we would decide later what to have for dinner. I offered juice to Michael, and he accepted it saying, "Yes, juice is better for you than soda." I asked him who told him that and he said his grandmother. He spoke very clearly and seemed to know what he wanted. Wesley and Stephen looked at each other and smiled. I knew then that having Michael around was going to be one of the best decisions we could have made. And that we had an exceptional little guy to raise was a plus.

As the day grew late, I prepared a quick dinner of chicken nuggets, mashed potatoes, and broccoli. Before long, it was time for Michael's bath. He loved taking baths and so I knew swimming lessons were to be added to our list of things to do for Michael. After bath time, I used baby lotion to keep Michael's extremely dry skin moist, and then took him to his bedroom. He loved his light blue colored bedroom with matching comforter and pillow set with colorful trains on them. Wesley came up to say good night and told Michael that he could call him "Uncle Wesley" and Michael smiled and said, "Good night, Uncle Wesley." I read a bedtime story to Michael and after I was finished reading, he looked at me and said "Good night, Mommy." My heart simply melted. The first day with us and Michael called me "Mommy." We thanked God for giving us such a special child. We were blessed to have Michael and he was blessed to have us.

Wesley and I made shopping plans for items Michael needed. Looking through the newspaper and flyers was enjoyable as we looked for coupons for Pampers, lotions, and baby powder for Michael's supply. Food shopping was different for us, as we looked to purchase certain food items that we thought Michael would prefer. We later learned that he enjoyed rice and fried chicken. I was not good at frying chicken, but was willing to give it a try. If my fried chicken was not tasty, then we would simply order fried chicken from a fast-food store.

With each passing day, Michael became more and more comfortable, and so did we. Working from home was ideal since I had a little one to look after. Everything was working out great and it was the height of summer, so I was looking forward to taking Michael to the playground after work hours.

It happened one afternoon after a long day of work. I decided we needed some fresh air, and it was a beautiful summer afternoon. I gathered up Michael and a few of his toys and a snack and buckled him safely in his car seat. We drove to a nearby playground. Michael's eyes lit up when we arrived because I didn't tell him where we were going, though he asked many times during the drive. He told me that his favorite thing at the playground was the sliding board. Up and down the stairs of the sliding board he went. He was having so much fun. Then it was time to leave the playground. When I warned Michael that he had ten minutes remaining, he was fine with it. However, when I informed him his ten minutes were up, he quickly ran towards the car which was parked in the parking lot. Michael ran around the car, all the while me screaming, "Stop!" I tried not to run but I was concerned that perhaps he was going to run out into the street. My heart was pounding so loud that if you were near me, I'm sure you would have heard it. Panic was taking over as I pleaded with Michael to come directly to me.

It seemed like time had stood still, but then Michael finally came towards me. I grabbed him and hugged him, all the while telling him never to run from me again. I explained to him that it was not a good feeling for me, and I was scared, and it was not safe for him to run from me. As young as he was, he apologized. When we got in the car, Michael's behavior turned to screaming, kicking and crying. I was shocked. What happened? In between his crying, he said he was not ready to leave the playground. I explained to him in a calm voice that the sun would be going down and it soon will be dinnertime. He screamed and kicked his feet on the back of the car seat during the short ride home. Somehow, I was able to block out his screams and crying and concentrate on driving safely home. I had our windows rolled down slightly just to get a little fresh air and hopefully help calm down Michael. Well, Michael took off his sneakers and socks and threw one sock out the car window! I was furious but said nothing.

When we arrived home, I literally had to pull him out of the car seat. He was still upset. Since he took off his shoes and socks, I let him walk barefoot on the warm cement sidewalk. He said, "Mommy, this ground is warm." And I replied, "Well, if you kept your sneakers and socks on, you would be more comfortable." I took him to his bedroom and informed him that he was in time-out because of his unacceptable behavior. Two minutes of standing in the corner was his time-out. I then slightly closed his bedroom door. He began screaming and crying loudly. I stood outside of his bedroom door for two minutes watching him. He was not calming down! I opened his bedroom door and looked at him without blinking an eye; he stared right back at me, not blinking, either! Oh my, I thought. So, this is the real Michael. Hmmmm. The screaming and crying went on for about an hour as he laid in his bed. I was beside myself and thinking, *What on Earth did I get myself into?* I then decided to use my phone camera to video his behavior. Afterwards, I showed him the video so he could see how awful he was behaving. It worked! He calmed down after he saw the video. He looked at me as if to say, "That's me acting crazy." I looked at Michael and said, "Yep, this is you not behaving nicely."

So, our sweet little intelligent Michael had a bad temper when he couldn't get his way. This was lesson number two — "Spare the rod, spoil the child." **Proverbs 13:24** says: **"He that spareth his rod hateth his son: but he that loveth him chasteneth him betimes."** If children are disciplined, and feel ashamed or sorrowful of their wrongdoing, it may become easier for them to ask Jesus to forgive them and be saved. Michael was warned that if he continued with that type of behavior, then there would be more time-out periods. After several time-out periods, I soon learned that Michael did not like to be left alone in time-outs. However, it took quite some time to break Michael out of his tantrum or terrible twos phase. As he got older, the tantrums dissipated.

In the months to come, raising Michael was an eye-opener, and we learned from him as much as he learned from us. One thing was for sure, you are never too old to learn. Raising Michael and coping with his tantrums created circumstances where it showed my patience, my strength and my ability and desire to teach. Each day, I would set aside a specific time in the mornings to educate Michael in reading, math and colors, and provide arts and craft time to amplify his creativity and imagination. Storybook time, which was just before bedtime, was proving to be beneficial as Michael began to pretend reading me the stories. Once Michael turned three years old, we decided to enroll him in a Pre-K program where he could be around other children his age. We felt it was time to develop his social and emotional behavior and continue to teach him to follow rules. Our conclusion was that a high-quality and full schedule of activities provided by a Pre-K program would only heighten Michael's intellect, because the few hours of my educating him at home simply was not enough.

Stephen, who Michael lovingly called Steve, looked after Michael at times. Stephen would take time when he got off from work to play roughhouse with Michael. Wesley would do the same. I disliked the roughhouse playing because I thought eventually, someone would get hurt — meaning Michael.

Nevertheless, the boys continued with the roughhousing games. Michael loved the attention from both Wesley and Stephen and the bond between the boys grew tighter and tighter as time progressed. I was no longer the center of Michael's life. Yes, I had been replaced by two males! No, I was not really replaced, nor was I jealous, but more so elated that the boys bonded. It made for such a happier home.

Regarding the roughhouse play, it gave Michael a "balance of protection" (more so from me) and "reasonable risk-taking" (from Wesley and Stephen) during their playtime. Mothers provide more of the nurturing, loving, kind, soft, gentle and protective atmosphere while fathers encourage the risk-taking, loud, or boisterous voice, challenges and rough play to young sons. Male figures provide or help instill the values required for young boys to become men. Also, they show love from a male perspective, so the child learns that it is natural to show emotions. According to research, having a positive male figure helps promote self-confidence and well-being. No matter how hard a mother tries to provide everything to a son, it is so important for a young boy to have a positive male presence in his life for the reasons I mentioned above. Of course, there exists many other reasons a positive male presence is important to a young boy (https://www.pediatricsoffranklin.com/resources-and-education/pediatric-care/the-importance-of-a-father-in-a-childs-life/).

One day, when Stephen, Michael and I were sitting at the kitchen table, out of nowhere, Michael asked whether Stephen was his big brother. *How do you answer that?* I thought. Stephen and I looked at each other with a puzzled look. In reality, this was not such an odd question. After all, Michael had "special names" for me and Wesley. Why not have a special name for Stephen? After a few minutes passed, I replied, "Yes, if you want to call him your 'big' brother, then so be it." A slow but wide grin was Michael and Stephen's response.

We knew it was fine for Michael to let us know what he wanted to call us because during one of our training sessions this very topic was discussed. Many foster parents wondered what name would be best for the fostered child to use. The instructor told us the child will make that decision based on his or her comfort level. Some foster children call the foster parents grandmom or granddad, auntie, uncle, mommy, etc. Now Michael had, as crazy as it might sound, "Mommy," "Uncle Wesley" and "Big Brother Stephen" as his additional family.

There were so many more "lessons learned" with Michael, but I will not take up the time to list them all. I am sure you can imagine how it can be raising a two-year-old going on six and having an already grown son. We raised Michael for two years. We celebrated each year with Michael's selection of a cartoon character. It is important to know that his mother, grandmother and cousin were all present at a second birthday celebration held at the social services agency center. It was standard policy for the biological mother and her child to have visits and celebrate special occasions together; however, it was not policy to have the entire family present. This went on for each occasion. I never complained about having the entire family present, nor did the social services agency enforce the policy. For me, it was whatever made Michael happy.

Michael's one-on-one visits with his biological mother made him happy, and by the time he was three years old, he knew exactly when visitation day was. There was one setback after Michael's visits with his biological mom — his behavior would revert, and the tantrums would resurface. It was a little draining for me since the visits were weekly. I had no choice but to cope with the idea of re-teaching him positive behavior. Of course, we loved Michael and would do anything for him; we continued to provide love, safety, security and nurturing. Then, our lives changed. We made another major decision.

CHAPTER 10

A Season of Change

As Wesley neared the age of 62, retirement was on the horizon. We discussed whether this would be a good time to take that big step. Policies and benefit packages were changing at his place of work, and my company had already completed an acquisition back in 2009, and was now owned by another company. The acquisition at my company caused most workers to be laid off or relocate. It was a difficult period, mostly for those at my company who did not have tenure with the company — no retirement package would be offered, rather only a two-week pay is what was rumored.

In looking at our financial situation, and the type of work Wesley did, we decided it was best for him to retire in January 2017. It was the best decision and he never regretted it. Wesley loved being in retirement. Oftentimes he would say how amazing it felt to receive his financial benefits monthly and not work for it. Though, in reality, we understood that he earned his benefits by working over 35 years at the same company.

My retirement happened eight years after the company's acquisition, in which the company I worked for had been sold. The first year after the acquisition there were many layoffs. Then in November 2016, another heralding, massive wave of layoffs began to sweep through the company globally. I believe the layoffs had a lot to do with the constant mergers and divestitures. Though we were inundated with projects, cuts had to be made. Employees were summoned in groups and informed that the company had designed multiple categories such as: those who were to be assigned to another location within the region, those who were not vested in the company, those who could relocate to Michigan (some of whom the company would pay relocation expenses and others to relocate at their own expense), those who were needed temporarily (two-year extension, then laid off) and lastly, those who were eligible for the separation package. My choice was a no-brainer.

With 41 years of service, and with the medical challenges I had dealt with, I took this as God's way of letting me know my work was finished at the company and it was now time for me to do whatever was my passion. For other employees, the news provided was heartbreaking. Many had families, children just starting college, mortgages and an array of different situations. As I looked around in the conference room, some employees were tearful, shocked or dismayed. The room went silent, and you could hear a pin drop; it was chilling as reality began to set in. My heart sank just to think of what my co-workers and friends were facing. I prayed that things would work in their favor.

After the summons was over, a small group of co-workers gathered to discuss the various options that were provided to us.

The discussion was focused on who thought who would fit into which category. Everyone knew the obvious decision for me to make. For others, it was like finger pointing, and each person stating what the best category was for the other. Naturally, most of them thought they were more important than the other. All the while, I'm thinking, whether or not they realized it, the decision for us was already made. The company, I felt, knew who they wanted to keep permanently, temporarily, who to lay off and who would probably accept the separation/retirement package. I had no qualms about accepting the separation package. Yes, the company decided to make changes, but God had a plan for us all.

God's timing is perfect. At the right time, He will provide what we need. **"But I trusted in thee, O Lord: I said, Thou art my God. My times are in thy hand: deliver me from the hand of mine enemies, and from them that persecute me" (Psalm 31:14-15).** The job was not my enemy, but I needed time to rest and reflect on my previous challenges, trials and tribulations, so that I could meditate and praise God for my health and strength. It was a time when both Wesley and I could make certain that God, and He alone, gets the glory and praise for pulling us through our difficult situations. I needed to slow my pace and give more attention to Wesley and allow the two of us to enjoy more time together. God was allowing us to enjoy the harvest together as we both sowed our seeds.

Holding down a job and raising a family certainly will keep you busy, and you hardly have any time for yourself. Easier said than done, but it is important to spiritually reflect on God's greatness and invite Him in our moments of meditations. When you take time to spiritually reflect, you are quieting your spirit man (meditating), and purposefully allowing the Holy Spirit to speak to you and guide you. When you have emptied out your mind, it can be replaced with God's love and His purpose for your life. God has a plan for all of us. We just need to listen, be obedient and make God a priority daily. This brings me to the scripture, **"Be still, and know that I am God: I will be exalted among the heathen, I will be exalted in the earth" (Psalm 46:10).**

I accepted my retirement package on March 31, 2017. Wesley came down to the job with me to sign off on my retirement package. We were both filled with excitement and ready to head out to my retirement luncheon that my manager and friend prepared. We celebrated at a nearby restaurant, making it convenient for family and friends. Everyone was genuinely happy for us, and speeches were given, photos taken along with many well-wishes. It was one of the happiest moments in my life. It was time for me to move on to another chapter in my life. Imagine, now I got to do whatever I wanted, whenever I wanted.

Spending time at home with Wesley, Stephen and Michael was fantastic! No longer did I have to worry about whether my phone was on mute so my co-workers could not hear Michael in the background. No more rushing home from the daycare to dial into a conference call. There were many mornings when Wesley and I would sit at the kitchen table having breakfast and conversing while looking out the patio door. Our conversations always turned to be about how the Lord had blessed us to be happily married and to be able to enjoy our retirement together. We both were healthy and grateful for that. Stephen was moving up the corporate ladder, making us even more proud to be his parents. Life was wonderful.

My passion had always been to become a teacher, and being a foster parent to Michael opened my mind more to the possibility of fulfilling this desire. Taking Michael to the Pre-K program offered for his age group and conversing with his teachers only heighted my desire. At dismissal time for the students, his teachers would take time to talk with me to inform me of Michael's day, and share their responsibilities with me to encourage me to apply for a position in their organization. I had to wait for the right time. I had no idea on when or how the "right" time was going to happen, but it did!

In August 2017, the social services agency contacted us and informed us they had a couple who wanted to adopt Michael, which broke our hearts. It was explained that Michael was age three now, which was a prime age to be adopted. Wesley, Stephen and I struggled with the fact of Michael leaving us. We pondered the idea of adopting him ourselves, but we felt we were too old to adopt. It was one of the most difficult decisions we had to make. We were a family, and everything was going great. How could the social services agency uproot a perfectly happy child from a sound environment, just like that? We were informed that Michael would spend the weekend with the prospective couple to ensure it would be a good fit. Michael cried as he left to spend the weekend with the couple. Two weeks had gone by, and the decision was final; Michael was leaving us to live with his new parents-to-be. It was a gloomy day, not physically, but in our hearts. As we packed everything Michael owned into the small car the caseworker drove up in, it became harder to hold back the tears.

We packed Michael's personal book which I used to make daily entries about Michael's progress, activities and basically things we thought he would like to know about when he grew older. We also included his photo album from birthday parties and trips we took him on, such as visits at the zoo and museums, and school photos. We hoped that from these photos, Michael would be able to look back and see how much fun he had, and how much he was loved. Oh, how we regretted the decision we made not to adopt him. We missed Michael!

Becoming a foster parent for us was worth it and we miss giving love, a safe home and security to a child in need — Michael. The new parents promised to keep in touch, and we thought we would be the grandparents; but they did not keep their promise. There were only a few contacts made, questioning me on how best to handle Michael when he had tantrums. I willfully provided different tactics. The last conversation we had with his new parents was that Michael was not adjusting well and the psychologist thought it best that he does not contact us anymore. That is when the phone calls stopped. No more calls with questions on how to handle a particular situation. No more calls to "Mommy," "Uncle Wesley" and "Big Brother Stephen." We made phone calls to the new parents, but no answer. We just felt a need to keep in touch, at least with the new parents, not necessarily to be able to actually speak with Michael.

Life without Michael was somewhat uneventful, and we all felt the void he left. Wesley and I started having movie night dates on Tuesday evenings, which just happened to be senior discount days. If it wasn't too late, we would stop and have dinner at a local restaurant after the movies. To help fill the void, I became more engulfed in various duties at my church, which included becoming the senior choir directress, and attended more of the special events or services held at church.

CHAPTER 11

Don't Give Up:
Help is on the Way

In the late evenings, Wesley and I would have popcorn while watching a movie at home. There would be a few times when Stephen would join us on our dinner outings, but mostly, he had to work late and arrived home in the early morning hours. Our life continued down this path until two months later, when I decided I needed a change of pace. I was bored. Several conversations took place with Wesley on how he felt about what I was planning. And, of course, he agreed and said, "Whatever makes you happy, babe." I prayed about it and read and reread about the responsibilities I was about to embark upon.

Since it has been what seemed a long time (approximately two months) without Michael, and me being retired with too much time on my hands, this was the perfect time to apply at an education services agency in my region. At first, I applied for a substitute teaching position, and then a few days later I decided to apply for an assistant instructor position. Quickly, I wrote my resume, which I never had to do, and submitted my application. The very next day, I received a phone call requesting me to come in for an interview. I only had two days to prepare for the interview. I accepted and immediately did research on the types of questions they may ask an assistant instructor for Pre-K.

The day of my interview was nerve-wracking. When I arrived, I was given the job description document, which I read and reread until the secretary asked for it back. Just like I thought, I was going to be tested on what I read. Unbeknownst to me, there were two sets of interviews I was subjected to. The first set was with two of the educator coordinators, and yes, they drilled me on the job responsibility document and my experience working with children. The second interview session was given by their boss and her assistant. It was a tough interview and basically was based on what-ifs and school safety rules. Afterwards, thinking I was done with the interviews, I was asked to provide a writing sample and told where to exit once I completed my writing sample. By this time, my hands were shaking but I managed to calm down enough to write the one-page sample. I was so nervous that I forgot the direction on how to exit the area and had to ask directions for the way out; it was different than the way I entered. I was so embarrassed.

As I walked to my car, still nervous, I focused on how I thought the interviews went. The research I had done on possible questions asked during an interview for the position did prove fruitful. I sat in my car and concluded that I could have done better. After the drilling of questions, I felt that I deserved the job and I really wanted it. The next day, I was offered the position and told to come to the office to sign papers and be assigned to my location.

My only question to them was, "Why not place me at the location nearest to my home?" The response was that I was placed where I was needed.

I was ecstatic on receiving the offer, though the pay was low, but again this was not a job, but my passion. Thank you, Jesus, for hearing my prayers! Wesley and Stephen were so happy for me because I got to do what I had always wanted to do.

I was assigned to one of the two Pre-K locations where the organization rented classrooms in a public elementary school building. The other Pre-K locations were located at various centers. I started working on Columbus Day in October 2017. I loved working with my lead instructor, and of course, I was excited and loved working with the students. Learning how to conduct the class was awesome. Teaching Pre-K was largely about being on a routine schedule, learning the different behaviors of each student and teaching and allowing the students to communicate their feelings. Before I knew it, the time to prepare for graduation was upon us. In the month of May, all instructors were giving thought on the graduation program. A few songs and individual acknowledgement of all students and instructors from each location would be the highlight.

The day of graduation, most students were dressed in their fine summer outfits and plenty of photos were taken. The parents thanked instructors for their support and for patience with working with their child. For me, it was truly an honor to work with the students and it was pleasing to see their progress. After the graduation ceremony, the instructors were provided lunch, and then we bid farewell until the next school year.

It was during the next school term (2018) that my lead teacher accepted another position (a promotion for her). One day prior to the class starting, the two of us were in the classroom preparing for our students when the class phone rang. When my lead instructor answered, she informed me that the call was for me. Of course, I was surprised and wondered who would be calling me at school, as I had informed Wesley that he could call my cell phone if he ever needed to reach me.

Lo and behold, it was a job offer for the lead instructor position! They wanted me to replace my lead instructor. When I informed my lead instructor about it, she commented saying that our location needed someone with a lot of experience! *Hmmm*, I thought, *so she didn't think I was qualified!* Obviously, they thought I was, and her comment only made me want the position that much more. I accepted.

Little did I realize, I had to apply online and provide an updated resume to fit the qualification criteria as a lead instructor. I had to go through the interview process all over again. The same two educator coordinators interviewed me, and this time I was less nervous.

I was accepted as the lead instructor at my same location, which was a blessing. Later, I found out that my location was one of the best, and other instructors wanted to be assigned here, too. I was temporarily assigned with an assistant for two months, which did not work out. It simply was not a good fit, and I was relieved when finally, my permanent assistant was assigned. Again, God had done it, hearing my prayers for an assistant that loved her job. Ms. Josephine (not her real name) had a great personality and was wonderful to work with. Our students connected with us, and we only had two students who had behavioral concerns. We managed and had a successful school year.

The following school year, September 2019, an assistant from a different location requested to work with me. She had more tenure than Ms. Josephine, so Ms. Josephine was re-assigned to another location, and I now had a new assistant. It was a bittersweet departure. A new school year and a new assistant, but all in all, we hit it off good. I could see that my new assistant, Ms. Dawn (not her real name), was eager to teach the class. Therefore, we balanced some of the teaching, using her strong point in art to work with the students. She loved assisting with the homework assignments amongst other things. The school year ended great, and things were great until I scheduled and had my annual flexible sigmoidoscopy procedure on August 16, 2019. I was up against another health challenge.

The result from my flexible sigmoidoscopy procedure showed that I had a "carpet-like" spread of polyps located in my rectum. The bottom line was that I had to have my rectum removed! What was God trying to tell me? I was doing what I always wanted to do. I was not hurting anyone. I was working in my church, as the senior choir directress, the church administrator, the event coordinator and I was paying my tithes. I just couldn't fathom why God was trying to get my attention. Was there some deep-down sin that God wanted to cleanse me of? I do believe that God needs to break us down for us to depend on Him completely and solely. Hadn't I already been broken and put back together, all the while trusting in Him? After what the Lord had already done for me, there was no way of me turning away from Him. I was grateful, faithful, prayerful and a God-fearing Christian. I was more than happy to give my testimony of His miracles. My trials definitely came in multiples! Hadn't I been through enough? I could only think that the Lord wanted to refine, restore, and purify me and continue to use me as that "today's miracle" that I mentioned at the beginning of my story. Be careful what you ask for and remember that God does not need any instructions from us!

There are people just like me who are wondering what it is that God is trying to tell them, or why He is trying to get our attention. Or perhaps you have come to a place in your life where circumstances are piled up and you just can't take any more; you are about to break. And you ask, "Why all the hurt and pain?" I have no answers, but what I do know is that "God's purpose is not of defeat, but of restoration." Throughout the Bible, the Lord offers hope when all else fails. In going through my health issues, I had to believe and have hope that my health would be restored, and as the Word of God says, **"For I will restore health unto thee, and I will heal thee of thy wounds, saith the LORD; because they called thee an Outcast, saying, This is Zion, whom no man seeketh after" (Jeremiah 30:17).**

Having hope is the desire to come out of an unpleasant circumstance or situation so your life can become better. Hope motivates us to make the necessary decisions or take the steps needed to move toward the visions of what we see as better; for example, a better future or greater happiness. It is having an expectation and anticipation of a positive or desired outcome. When we have hope, we believe that good things can still happen. As for me, my energy is placed in faith and hope in God and believing He will work it out for my good. God will do just what

He said He would. God speaks of faith and hope in many scriptures. **Job 11:18 says, "And thou shalt be secure, because there is hope; yea, thou shalt dig about thee, and thou shalt take thy rest in safety."** No matter how much thought we put into trying to figure out why we are faced with unwanted circumstances or situations, the bottom line is there is no rhyme or reason, but there is hope.

Moving past the figuring-out state of mind and into more of a spiritual mindset, it was then that I began to realize that for God to refine, restore and renew or purify me, I first had to be stripped of my "clothing" to get cleansed and rinsed. I had to be emptied of self for God to fill me with faith and hope and of His Spirit. It was necessary for me to empty all negativity and be thirsty for God because He can satisfy all our needs and fulfill our deepest desires. Changing my mindset was a major factor to help me realize that I needed to look back on all the wonderful miracles that God had previously performed in my life. As I reflect on this journey, I surround myself with family and friends, who were optimistic and persistently pushing and encouraging me, who are the kind of people you should associate with and soak up their positivity. I needed to be optimistic and inspired about my arduous journey. And my faith is a source of inspiration. God's word in **Matthew 5:6 says, "Blessed are they which do hunger and thirst after righteousness: for they shall be filled."** There is an old hymn entitled "Fill My Cup Lord," and the lyrics are:

FILL MY CUP LORD

Like the woman at the well
I was seeking
For things that could not satisfy
And then I heard my Savior speaking
"Draw from My well that never shall run dry"
Fill my cup, Lord
I lift it up, Lord
Come and quench this thirsting of my soul
Bread of Heaven, feed me 'til I want no more
Fill my cup, fill it up and make me whole
There are millions in this world
Who are craving
The pleasures, earthly things of gold
But none can match the wondrous treasure
That I find in Jesus Christ my Lord
Fill my cup, Lord
I lift it up, Lord
Come and quench this thirsting of my soul
Bread of Heaven, feed me 'til I want no more
Fill my cup, fill it up and make me whole
Here's my cup, fill it up and make me whole

Songwriter: Richard Blanchard, Sr.

My favorite is the second verse, and I could sing this repeatedly because it speaks to having such a thirst for the Lord that you want your cup to be full. It is my opinion that the lyrics mean to replenish and restore your mental state, your physical being and your emotional state. All I can say to this is, **"HALLELUJAH!"** Our God can do anything! God is able! Nothing is too hard for God!

Receiving the results that yet another surgery had to be performed, I grew accustomed to taking deep breaths to connect with the emotions that were rising inwardly. I would not allow my shock and disappointment in the results overrule me. There were no tears, simply the "I gotta go through this again" and "God is not through with me yet" attitude. I think perhaps I had become dull to hearing the word "surgery."

The 2019 school year was beginning, so I focused on preparing my classroom and reading through each student's file. My assistant instructor, Ms. Dawn, helped with decorating the classroom. I did as much work as I possibly could so as not to think about having a consultation with yet another doctor.

Wesley and I were referred to a specialist in colon, rectal and anal diseases. Our appointment was set quickly, as time was against us and we did not want things to get worse. On October 1, 2019, we met one of the nicest, kindest and most gentle surgeons that one could ever meet. Wesley and I immediately felt comfortable with the colorectal surgeon. When I informed the colorectal surgeon of my history and that I had another colorectal surgeon who worked in the same field, he let me know he would not be offended if I changed surgeons. We did not take offense to this because of how he said it — soft and gentle. And it was just an option. We felt that the Lord led us to this surgeon and therefore, we would stick with him.

The colorectal surgeon received all my medical history and was warned of adhesions (scar tissue) in my stomach area that were "made of steel," according to my previous surgeon. This information regarding the adhesions proved to be particularly important for the upcoming surgery. My surgery date was set for October 30, 2019. In preparation for the surgery, notification and forms were forwarded to the Human Resource Department at my job. Informing Ms. Dawn, my assistant, of the news that I would be on medical leave was difficult. For whatever reason, I sensed that though she desired to take the lead in teaching, she showed some reluctance when the situation presented itself.

Two weeks passed, and still there was no information from my supervisor on who would be my fill-in during my medical leave. With each passing day, I diligently showed Ms. Dawn more responsibilities as a lead instructor. And it was time to share the news about my medical leave with Ms. Dawn, which would give her two weeks to accept her new challenge. Ms. Dawn genuinely was concerned, devastated and stunned upon hearing the news that it was estimated that I would be on medical leave for three months. I did not share with her the details regarding the surgery; that was too personal, and I was still coping with the fact that I was having yet another surgery, and would need to wear an ileostomy bag. Yes, I said it. An ileostomy bag due to having my rectum removed.

At the consultation with the colorectal surgeon, Wesley and I learned that the surgery would be two-fold. He would perform a proctectomy, which is the rectum removal, with a j-pouch and ileostomy. Once the rectum is removed, the body needs a way to eliminate waste. Therefore, the surgeon described this as the need to perform an ileostomy. An opening on the side of my abdomen would be made to make it so that part of the small intestine could be pulled through the opening enough to allow gas and waste to flow through into the ileostomy bag. The j-pouch would be the replacement of the rectum and would need time to heal before it would be able to perform the necessities. I know, too much information! Can you imagine how I felt? Recall when I had my colon removed, I literally freaked out at the thought of having to wear a bag. And now, it was inevitable.

Perhaps you are wondering how am I able to cope with so much pain and suffering? Or perhaps you have wrestled with your own challenges and wondered, why so much pain and suffering? My burdens are lightened knowing that when you believe in God, then you also believe in Jesus Christ our Lord who promised never to leave nor forsake us. **"Let not your heart be troubled: Ye believe in God, believe also in Me" (John 14:1).** Jesus is letting us know that He is trustworthy. As Christians, we will struggle, but trust Him and he will handle it for us. Jesus told his disciples, "Let not your heart be troubled." In other words, don't let your heart shake or quiver from trouble. He is there for us. Though we live in troubled times, Jesus tells us to not worry and turn our troubles over to him. **"Casting all your care upon him; for he careth for you" (I Peter 5:7).**

Just think about what we do when trouble strikes. Most people, I think, call on the name of Jesus in the time of trouble. It may be the only time His name is called. Our troubles and struggles will bring us to our knees, bowing down to God, praying for help. During our struggles and suffering, this could be how God gets us to trust in Him. He is, perhaps, getting our attention as a way of letting us know that we are not walking alone and to come to Him for He is our Father.

In my eyes, yes, I accept the Lord Jesus Christ as my personal savior, but that does not alienate me from suffering. I encourage myself to look past the suffering and believe that in some way, that in my suffering, a blessing is on the way! This keeps me focused and trusting in the Lord and knowing that my suffering was not caused by foolish choices, but rather from a hereditary family trait. It is important to know that, depending on choices we make, if foolish decisions are made, we will have to deal with the consequences. So, knowing that suffering can come from poor or foolish choices, it behooves us to make wise decisions. In **Proverbs 13:1-25,** it speaks about common sense and that those who have good judgement have better understanding, and learn that when using common sense, we win.

By using common sense, I was encouraged to push forward and believed that, through all of this, a blessing was on the way. I would have this surgery. I would come through the battle, and yes, with scars as proof, but I will have made it through another miracle and with another testimony. Can God do it? Will God do it? Yes, God can, and Yes God will! **Hallelujah!** I knew with all certainty that God is sovereign and there is always hope. Just keep the faith. As my pastor would say: "Help is on the way!" The Word of God tells us: **"Now faith is the substance of things hoped for, the evidence of things not seen" (Hebrews 11:1).**

The proctectomy and ileostomy surgery took longer than expected. The cause was due to the adhesions that the surgeon was warned about. It took an hour to cut through and remove those "made of steel" adhesions that were hindering the surgeon and his partner from getting to my rectum. The good thing is that they were made aware of them prior to the surgery. They did not, however, think that it would be as difficult as it was. They removed as many adhesions as they could.

There were no other complications during the surgery. Afterwards, I was placed in the recovery area and when I was somewhat coherent, I was informed that I did well. Upon hearing this, my first words were, "**Thank you Jesus**" and "**Hallelujah!**" When I fully recovered from the anesthesia, I thanked the Lord for being with me and bringing me thus far. I slept on and off, but was completely aware of where I was and what took place. One of my best girlfriends (I have two) came to visit hours after the surgery. She was amazed at how alert I was. Of course, I was on pain medication, so I did not feel any pain. However, I did check myself for the ileostomy bag. Yes, it was there.

On November 12, 2019, it was discovered that something was amiss in my abdomen. Those adhesions were causing an intestinal blockage. The surgeon and his associate performed a laparotomy exploratory, LOA, Enterotomy X1, Myotomy X2 surgery. From this point on, all I recall is being on pain medications and round-the-clock care by nurses and patient care technicians.

The nurses would come to check on my pain level and my ileostomy bag, which seemed to happen about every three hours. The patient care technicians would take my vitals and prick my finger approximately every two hours. Whatever the timeframes were, I could never get a full night of sleep. Even my naps were interrupted at the most inopportune time. One of the worst things about being in the hospital for me was when the intravenous pain medication drip was removed. Now I would have to request my pain medicine and provide a number describing the level of pain. How would I really know at what level of pain I was in? Therefore, my frequently used number was six. I would always ask for the last time my pain medicine was administered because I did not want to suffer pain where it would take more time for my body to react to the medicine. In other words, give me my pain medication before it reached a point of excruciating pain.

The second worst thing for me in the hospital was the ileostomy bag. I hated the fact that I had to wear it. And after a week of the nurse changing my ileostomy bag while in the hospital, it was time for me to learn. I absolutely dreaded the fact that I had to learn to change it myself, but I wanted to go home and had to learn to become independent. I was discharged from the hospital December 6, 2019. There is no need for me to go into details regarding what it was like having an ileostomy bag, just know it is something you do not ever want to go through. Dealing with it was hard, but determined as I was, I pushed myself to return to my job. So, after five months of constant in-home care visits from nurses, which included receiving TPN infusion for nourishment and walking around the house with a backpack to hold the TNP bag, I welcomed the change of environment. Wesley questioned my decision of returning to work, but I knew that I wanted to go back to my passion of teaching. It was a matter of getting back to normality.

Despite Wesley's concern, I was elated to be returning to my classroom in March 2020. Contacting Ms. Dawn to inform her of my pending return was an emotional moment for the both of us. In her voice, I could hear the relief and excitement regarding my return. Ms. Dawn provided me with an update on our students' progress, both behavioral development and academic progress.

After speaking with her, I began my preparation for the upcoming days.

There was excitement in the air upon the first day of my return from medical leave. Plenty of hugs, cheek kissing and enthusiastic greetings took place in the classroom from both the parents and my students. Trying desperately to hold back my tears, I tilted my head up slightly to keep the tears from streaming down my face. It did not work. My little students raced to get me a tissue. Too emotional to remind them to use their 'walking feet' (because it was safe), at that moment, I overlooked the possibility of them falling. Their reactions touched my heart and certainly made me feel missed and appreciated.

The following days were fruitful, and my students continued to be excited about my being back in motion. They learned to treat me with caution once they understood that due to my surgery, my stomach was still tender — only one parent knew about my ileostomy bag. On a few occasions, a student would forget and try to give me a big hug or bump their head against my stomach when sitting in my lap during Circle Time. I corrected that by instructing a student to sit with Ms. Dawn. School days were going well with little behavior issues and no accidents.

The Lord had allowed me to return to my passion and teach a wonderful group of students—for this, I was grateful. My adjustment to having the ileostomy bag took some getting used to, and I did have my problems with it. I learned not to eat before school started and eat little during lunchtime to diminish my need for bio breaks. At home, my meal portions were based on the amount I could consume, which was not much. I continued to have issues with my ileostomy bag, which at times would bring me to tears. I hated having it! Knowing that I should not dwell on the negative because it only makes the situation worse, I decided it was in my best interest to accept it and be grateful that the doctors have the knowledge and skill to perform a surgery such as this.

CHAPTER 12

Accepting the Unexpected

As if things in my life couldn't get any worse, I was presented with another chapter in my life of being overwhelmed and this time with bitterness, anger, loss, heartbreak and stress. **"...When my heart is overwhelmed: lead me to the rock that is higher than I" (Psalm 61:2).** I knew that no matter what stage of life or Christian walk we're in, we still will face adversities. This was much too much to accept! This could not be happening! I couldn't eat, sleep or concentrate. I could barely function. I felt lost and confused. I needed some answers. Everything was going great. I had just returned to teaching. Wesley and I were enjoying life together. We had our date nights and went out for dinner at times. Wesley enjoyed church services when he did finally go which was few and far between. And I had returned to my church responsibilities. At times I would have senior choir meetings at our house. Stephen was doing great at his job. Why was this happening to us?

It all began with noticing a repetition in asking the same question. At first, it went unnoticed, but it soon became clear that something was wrong. An appointment was made with the doctor who then scheduled an MRI after the failing of a short-term memory loss test. My eyes filled with tears as the doctor began to describe the possible cause. **UNBELIEVABLE!** I couldn't scream in the presence of Wesley, so I held it in until we arrived home. I told Wesley I needed to get some fresh air. Walking to the corner, I let out my frustrations by screaming. I didn't care what people thought. I was devastated. Wesley was devastated. Stephen was devastated.

The love of my life, my partner, my confidant, my lover, my soulmate, my husband, Wesley, was diagnosed with having a brain tumor. Why on Earth was this happening to us, or to him? He did not deserve this. Yes, I questioned God! Wesley was good people. How many times did something so awful happen to you or others you loved or to good people you know? Realistically, we know bad things happen to people no matter if you're good or bad. The common phrase of "God will not put more on you than you can bear" or "He will let you bend but you won't break" was not working for me.

This was a hard pill to swallow, and we felt crushed. Feeling as though my back was up against a wall, and at a loss for words, I wanted to fall to the floor and cry. How could we handle this unbearable weight? My answer was to pray. We all have or will be subjected to situations that seem unbearable. This type of news may cause a person to desperately seek different specialists no matter where they are located. It is during times such as this that we must fall to our knees to pray. For some, praying only comes when devastation come into our lives. However, there are always situations or someone that requires prayer.

Prayer is a weapon of power, and it is essential. My pastor taught us that when we (Christians) pray, it is in four basic forms: adoration; repentance; gratitude; and petition/intercession. And when we pray, we must believe and trust that God hears and will answer our prayers when our will is the will of God. In other words, our will must be aligned with God's will. God's will be done. In praying, we must be patient for God's answer and not get tired or faint. The word of God tells us: **"Even the youths shall faint and be weary, and the young men shall utterly fall: but they that wait upon the LORD shall renew their strength; they shall mount up with wings as eagles; they shall run, and not be weary; and they shall walk, and not faint" (Isaiah 40:30-31).** My prayer was a prayer of intercession for my husband. A prayer requesting complete healing.

Wesley encouraged me to go to work and said that he would be fine. Family members took turns spending days with Wesley while I went to work, which made me feel more secure. I did not want him in the house alone. Their visits helped take his mind off the surgery. The surgery was set for March 9, 2020.

Another unfortunate fact was this was during the onset of coronavirus (Covid-19). The death rate was already past 4,000 in the United States. The outbreak worsened across Europe and every country had a case of the virus according to news reported by CNN. And CNN had named coronavirus a "pandemic" (https://www.cnn.com/2020/03/10/world/newsletter-coronavirus-03-10-20-intl/index.html).

Due to what was now being called the coronavirus pandemic, hundreds of thousands of people had died from Covid-19 by mid-March 2020, and therefore, visits to the hospital were limited

(https://jamanetwork.com/journals/jamainternalmedicine/fullart
icle/2767980). Me, Stephen and a few other family members were
permitted to sit in the waiting area of the hospital during Wesley's
surgery.

After six hours of surgery, Wesley was taken to the
Neurological Intensive Care Unit, which the normal
procedure. Of course, prayers were going up on Wesley's behalf,
and we were all relieved when he came through. Praising God for
His mercy and for honoring my heart's desire, Wesley was in
stable condition. Wesley was not aware of where he was which was
not too alarming since he just came out of surgery. The next day,
Stephen and I visited Dad, who was talking and alert. Praise God!

As the days progressed, constant updates on Wesley's
condition were provided via phone calls. The pandemic had
gotten worse globally and thousands of more people were dying.
The spread of Covid-19 caused the hospital to enforce more strict
visitation rules. Wesley's condition was up and down. Feeling lost
and helpless, and now wondering whether my prayers were being
answered, I cried myself to sleep every night after praying that the
Lord step in and turn the situation around.

Wesley's condition was worsening. All I could do was to
continue praying. I contacted our "prayer warriors," begging them
to pray that Wesley pull through. I contacted my pastor who came
up to the hospital with us. I wanted my husband to live. I was
willing to do whatever was needed to have him here with me. God
saw it differently. The love of my life got his wings the morning of
March 23, 2020. There are no words on how I can describe my
feelings, Stephen's feelings nor his first-born son's feelings.

To say the least, Stephen and I were devastated, angry and filled with unbelief. It felt like an earthquake that shook and the cracks swallowed our world. Besides losing the love of my life, my son lost his father and best friend. Our lives will never be the same. Spiritually, for a short period of time, I felt like God had given me false hope, because one day Wesley's condition was like a see-saw, it went up and then it went down permanently. However, I remembered the most important thing about our prayers: they must be aligned with God's will, and not our will. God saw it best to take my husband. Naturally, I did not accept this initially. After all, I am human and loved my husband dearly. My heart was and still is broken. The realization hit me hard and decisions needed to be made on how we could have a funeral during the pandemic. The state began issuing regulations on how to safely have funerals, weddings and any other large gatherings.

Some of our family members found it difficult to comprehend the seriousness of the pandemic and how dangerous it would be to have the normal size funeral or memorial service. Either that or they were not keeping up with the news media or not accepting or not in agreement with the mandated regulations that were enforced regarding large crowds, distancing, wearing masks and handwashing. Their wish was to have a large memorial service in the middle of a pandemic! It was not safe, and the funeral director was not going to go against regulations and risk losing his funeral license. Anyway, it was not about them. Regardless of what was wanted, the fact remained that I lost my husband, the father of my son, and there would not be the homegoing service he deserved. I am sure there are many, many others who have gone through the same turmoil as myself. It was mandated that only ten people could attend funeral services! The question was, when would we be able to have a proper memorial service?

Nearing the end of 2020, Covid-19 continued to cause millions of deaths around the globe. Those who lost loved ones were still limited with the number of guests allowed at funeral services and face mask wearing and social distancing were enforced. Social media was now being used for "live" showings of the viewing (of the body) and used widely by many families.

I would like to share with you how wonderful Wesley was and how he was such an amazing and loving husband. Wesley would always ensure that I had everything and anything I needed, or wanted for that matter. He was a person who believed in taking care of everything in our house, except for the trash. That was Stephen's job. Stephen and Dad had such a loving bond, which made me so proud of them both. Dad loved being at home with his family. He enjoyed visits with other family members.

Cooking, cleaning and doing the laundry and ironing were household chores he loved to do. Hey, I did some cooking, too! Wesley also loved shopping online. I was his queen and "Lady Love" (song by Lou Rawls) as he affectionately called me, and he was my king. He helped teach me to be the woman I am today.

As I mentioned about cooking being a household chore — not really, it was not a chore but a pleasurable thing for him. Every Thanksgiving, he would kindly ask me what dishes we were going to prepare. That was my cue to create the menu and plan our cooking strategy. For you see, he had his 'special' dishes and I had mine. We cooked for approximately 20-25 people. Our guests did not show up all at the same time, and we made sure to prepare enough so they could take platters home for later. Thanksgiving was our favorite time of the year.

Wesley's cooking went further than just at Thanksgiving. We would have holiday cookouts with all the various BBQ foods and a bushel of blue crabs. Our cookouts became so popular that a few of our friends began calling and asking what day and time or when we were having our next cookout. When our friends began asking, I think that's when we gave second thoughts about having cookouts! Our last cookout was over at Jan's house. I don't recall why, but perhaps we wanted a different scenery, and she has a big yard.

Wesley loved singing. He had a smooth, sultry, sexy voice and sang every day at home, in the car, when we were with friends and anywhere, anytime. As for sports, he was a Dallas Cowboys fan and filled almost every room in our house with Cowboys memorabilia.

Wesley met no strangers. If you were standing next to him, there was something about him that drew you to him. You would have to have a conversation with him. He was so approachable and kind. Everywhere we went, somebody knew Wesley. His ties to his job led to many friendships and close ties to his 'boys' that continued until his demise. Wesley made every attempt to maintain the family bonds and relationships. He was the glue in the family that formed those bonds. There is so much more that I could share with you about him. The love of my love can never be replaced. There is not another like Wesley Gregg, Sr.

Death, I believe, can bring out the worst in people. And unfortunately, when there is death in a family, you may find out that there are those who you thought would be there for you who are not. You realize that they only think of themselves and material things that they can gain. Some people have no regard or are so insensitive that they will ask for personal items that belonged to your loved one on the same day of your loss! And, as for phone calls to see how you are doing from an insensitive person, well, forget that. The insensitive people won't even call. The way to handle those people is to check your cell phone directory, and simply press the delete button on those names. I believe that when God removes those who mean you no good from your life, do not go back and pick them up again. This may sound harsh, but it is better to be healthy and live with as little stress as possible.

As I mentioned before, many people, like myself, suffered the loss of a loved one during the early onset of the pandemic when safety regulations were being enforced and the death rates continued to climb. The pandemic denied proper homegoing services for many families. The pandemic also denied people the time to come together to grieve and provide or give support and even tell of stories about our loved one. Missing the physical hugs and the comforting words of sympathy made it that much harder for the grieving families. Hearing sympathy cards read during a funeral reaffirms that your life has changed but life continues, and that you are not alone in your sorrow. The reading aloud gives you comfort.

During the pandemic, some people used social media to share funeral or memorial services and view posted condolences; in my opinion, there is no comparison like receiving a personal, handwritten sympathy card stating what they remembered about your loved one. No matter how sympathy is received, though, it does help ease some of the pain. In our sorrow and grief, we need comfort and support long after the homegoing service. When a crisis is apparent or when you have lost a loved one, and weeks go by, are family members and friends still around?

I thank God for the comfort and support, especially from my sisters Lin and Jan, who took turns staying with Stephen and me in our time of sorrow. They spent several weeks with us and saw to it that we ate and got the rest we needed. And thanks to a friend, my pastor's brother, who provided delicious baked goodies. Thanks to close friends, my pastor and my church family for being there for us. I really don't think I would be where I am today without their support. When grieving, support from those who love you gives you the opportunity to share memories, giving you that sense of peace. I am not a grief counselor, but I believe it's important to be able to talk about your emotions, which may help prevent loneliness and even illnesses. And talking helps heal the hurt of losing a loved one.

Though it was difficult, Stephen returned to his job about one week after the death of his father. The family encouraged him to return to work because they could see that it was literally tearing him apart. Being in his room alone day in and day out was not healthy. Sure, Stephen and I would talk about Dad and cry together, but he needed to be kept busy. And I needed to be kept busy. Make no mistake about it, we were not avoiding the needed time to grieve. We knew we would be grieving for most of the rest of our life. My husband was everything to us. Our family was us!

Of course, we knew all about the grieving stages of denial, anger, bargaining, depression and acceptance. And a friend of ours is a grief counselor whom I did speak with several times. So, we did not need a lecture on whether it was too soon to return to work, or whether we needed more time and so on. There is no time set on grieving or when it's the right time to return to your regular activities. The loss of my husband will take a huge adjustment in my life and there is no way of knowing when the hurt and pain will cease.

CHAPTER 13

Broken But Not Shattered

For me, I didn't want to impose on my sisters any longer, and knew that eventually I would have to face being alone without my husband. In two weeks, I informed them of how much I loved and appreciated them, but it was time for me to get myself back to teaching. It would be a stress reliever for me, and I needed something else to fill my mind up with. And so, I returned to teaching in the month of April, but things there were different due to Covid-19. No longer were classes being held in the school building. My instructions upon returning were to pick up my school laptop and upload a teaching tool that would be used by parents and students. Class would now be held virtually.

The connection that Ms. Dawn and I had remained intact. We picked up where we left off and all went well. Class lessons were posted and reviewed by us. The tool we used allowed the students to video themselves as instructed per homework assignments. This was gratifying because at least we got a chance to see them, though physical presence is more beneficial for both teacher and student in my opinion. Virtual teaching continued for the remainder of the school year.

The June 2020 graduation ceremony was presented virtually. Teachers were instructed to gather pictures taken from different school activities and present a PowerPoint presentation. The presentations were uploaded in our teaching tool, enabling parents and students to view them on the official day of graduation. Sadly, that ended our June 2020 school year, and then it was on to another chapter of my life.

Finally, it was time for my ileostomy reversal surgery. My surgery was scheduled for July 17, 2020, and to last approximately two hours. The plan was for me to be hospitalized for no longer than five to seven days. Yes, there is a 'but' coming. For whatever reason, when I had surgery, nothing seemed to go as planned. There always seemed to be underlining situations that occurred, leaving my surgeons puzzled. I was always a unique situation. Hold on, don't stop reading. There is another testimony on the way.

The surgery went smoothly and as planned. I was recuperating and was getting my appetite back but, unfortunately, I was not allowed to eat anything yet. There was a tube inserted through my nostril down to my abdomen. It was uncomfortable so much that I hated to swallow my saliva or even to speak. Therefore, I kept quiet for the most part. Both my surgeon and his associate would take turns checking on me every morning and check on whether they heard gas build up in my abdomen. Nope, no sounds at all. There was no feeling of me needing to pass gas or desire to eliminate waste, which is important. Passing or hearing gas bubbles in my abdomen would confirm that my organs were functioning properly. Days passed by, and yet no feeling or hearing of gas bubbles.

About the fifth day, as my surgeon was using the stethoscope, I looked straight at him. I could see the concern on his face. It looked like he wanted to cry. I was scared! My surgeon informed me that he was going to schedule an MRI immediately because it was highly likely there was a blockage. I said in a calm voice, "Okay, what time tomorrow?" His response was, "I'm sorry, it will be scheduled for some time this morning." He informed me it was probably the adhesions that couldn't be reached that were causing the blockage. The MRI would show the exact cause of the problem. He said, "I'm so sorry you have to go through this." I said in my mind, *Yes, me too!* Geeze, here I go again. Instead, I simply responded by smiling and saying, "I'm just not the average patient." And I told him that I know he regrets taking me as his patient and if he knew it was going to be difficult, he would have referred me elsewhere. Of course, he denied it. Him denying it didn't make me feel any better; I still wanted to cry. I mean, really boo-hoo. But I didn't. I remained strong. At this point, I just thought, it is what it is. Knowing that God is the Chief Physician and Commander in Chief, I was not without hope. I was in perfect hands — again.

I called Stephen, Jan and Lin to give them the update. They were encouraging but behind the façade, I knew they were disappointed and hurt too. Time moved quickly, and before I could take a nap, the hospital orderly came to take me for my MRI. Hours later, my surgeon and his associate visited me to inform me that there was a blockage and surgery was set for July 24th; it would be a laparotomy lysis of adhesions-small bowel bypass. They promised that we would get through this. My surgeon told me to continue to pray to God because prayer seems to work! He was such a nice person and obviously aware that I believed in God.

From what I was told by both my surgeon and his associate, during the surgery, they had to call in another surgeon for advice regarding the removal of the adhesions. They had already removed many of them but needed to know if they should continue. The surgeon told them it was too risky to continue, and it was his advice to "close her up." Prayerfully, the number of adhesions removed this time would be enough for my bodily functions to work properly.

As I lay in my hospital bed, my thoughts focused on going home. I missed being able to rest and relax in my own bed. Mostly, I missed sitting at home with my husband planning our daily activities and hearing about our son's workday. Sadly, that would be no more. The days in the hospital turned into weeks as we waited for my muscles and bodily functions to begin to wake up and work. My doctors were patient as they did not want to perform another surgery, and I did not want to be put under anesthesia again. At my age of 61, I felt that each surgery was that much more dangerous; I was no longer a young woman. I wondered how much more could my body take.

My doctors thought I was such a good sport in how I was handling the news when they would tell me when more tests were needed or when another surgery was necessary. What was I to do? All I knew to do was to pray. There was no sense in throwing a tantrum, screaming or being a difficult patient. Often, I thought of the song entitled, "Take Your Burdens to The Lord, and Leave It There." This song reminded me that God will sustain me through times of trouble and weariness when I make my requests known to him, and to thank Him in advance for giving me peace and protection. No longer should I feel anxious over anything.

A promise of God that gives me daily strength is the biblical verse: **"Cast thy burden upon the Lord, and he shall sustain thee; he shall never suffer the righteous to be moved" (Psalm 55:22).** Lord knows, I needed some relief and a lightening up of my heavy burdens. No matter what burdens we have, God can bear them. God just doesn't want one burden but all our cares. It is not too much for Him.

My situation was getting to be too much for me, so I needed to take my burdens to the Lord and leave them with Him. I was determined not to allow tears or self-pity or depression to creep and lay dormant in my life. In my situation, there was no choice but to remain calm, quiet, prayerful and hopeful, and keep my thoughts on getting better so I could go home. Again, my caring sister, Jan, constantly gave updates of my condition to my pastor and prayer warriors.

As I grew stronger while in the hospital, I would listen to my pastor preaching on Sundays via social media. During the intercessory prayer, I would hear my name called. Knowing my church family and friends were lifting my name up in prayer made me feel confident that everything was going to be alright. After all, the Lord had these doctors in place, and my pastor, church family, sisters and friends all on one accord, praying for me.

After weeks in the hospital, the nurse conducting her normal routine came in to check on me, and just by chance, she decided to check my canister. I had a canister that had a tube connected to me to help eliminate fluid from my stomach. The hope was that eventually there would only be a small amount, which would be an indication that the tube could be removed. Lo and behold, there was a small amount of fluid in the canister! We all rejoiced. Can you imagine, we are in a hospital, and they are jumping up and down, being somewhat loud, bending over to hug me and congratulating me! It was all good, though. It was God showing up on my behalf. I was elated because that meant the tube in my nostril was coming out.

There was one minor setback that occurred a few days later. As I laid in my hospital bed watching television, there was a hissing sound prompting me to lift my blanket. Looking down at my stomach, I saw fluid seeping from my incision. Not panicking, I signaled for a nurse. It only took a minute or two for a nurse to appear. Showing her my stomach, she placed a covering over my incision and then reported it to my surgeon. The nurse was kind and encouraged me to not worry. Upon my surgeon's arrival, he looked at me and simply shook his head. I shrugged my shoulders as if saying, "Oh well." He described it as having an abdominal fistula, which can happen after abdominal surgery. The treatment was to be on antibiotics, continue with being on a feeding tube and wear a pouch to capture the discharge of fluid from my abdomen. The good news was that the tube in my nostril was being removed.

Neglecting to inform Stephen and Jan that I needed to have a pouch that was similar to the ileostomy bag, they were shocked upon seeing the pouch when they were allowed visitation. I reassured them that it was temporary and as my body healed, the abdominal fistula would close by itself. After all this drama, finally I was released and headed for home on August 13, 2020, with a laundry list of required medicines and instructions. Feeling relieved and knowing that I was, for sure, homeward bound, sleep came easy that night.

Recovery at home proved to be exactly what I needed. The gas and bubbling in my stomach were not evident while in the hospital but can I tell you that on the third day at home, my bowel activities began to function! All I can say is, "Won't He do it?" There were, of course, TPN and heparin flushes that I had to endure on a 12-hour period. Jan and Stephen helped administer the TPN and heparin flushes daily. With each monthly visit to the doctor, there was much improvement. The abdominal pouch was eventually removed with no other complications. The abdominal fistula eventually closed.

Covid-19 was still running rampant, but schools were partially opening and giving parents the choice of having virtual or in-class sessions for their child/children. Missing my students, I discussed with my surgeon about the possibility of returning to work. He looked at me as if I had four heads. No way would he agree it was time for me to return, especially with the pandemic and the number of deaths growing exponentially. Therefore, fortunately or unfortunately, depending on how you look at it, I had no choice but to retire. It was not logical to put myself in danger's way after all that I had been through, and the fact that I was still grieving and missing my husband while dealing with complications from my recent surgery. It was still hard for me to accept that he was gone. The year 2020 is one that many of us will never forget.

Being home was bittersweet. Though it was a blessing, the fact remained there was no Wesley to welcome me home. The memories were there, but I continued to grieve over my loss. Losing Wesley exacerbated my realization that life was too short.

At my age of 61, there was no time to procrastinate. I made the decision to work on living my life proactively versus reactively, and to do more things that are tuned to my passion. One thing I am learning about being alone is to cut toxic people out of my life. I no longer need or can tolerate negative people. My girlfriend and I have a saying: "Keep it moving." My life experiences profoundly affect how I will now live my life. Loneliness remains a part of me, and I prefer being by myself. Obviously, loneliness is not healthy, and I realize that I cannot not stay in this funk. Still, I was not ready to "keep it moving."

Being a widow feels awkward and incomplete. Friends have asked whether I'd considered dating, or do I think it's time to move on? Move on? It had only been one year since the loss of my husband, and I did not feel that it was fair for my friends to put pressure on me about dating. There is no specific set time for mourning or when to start dating when you become a widow or widower. Well, maybe I do need a change of pace, but dating? Nah. Yes, I still get lonely, that's for sure, but after 39 years of marriage, it's hard to move on, especially when death came in such a short time.

The evenings and nights are the worst times for me. That's when the feeling of loneliness hits hardest. During the day is when I experience incredibly high level of stress. Though now loneliness has become a huge part in my life, dating is not in my vocabulary.

Feeling like a broken or cracked vessel, though my vessel did not break into a million pieces, but my heart felt that way, I am still encouraged. At times I say to myself, "Broken but not shattered." It makes no difference whether you feel like you have been broken into a million pieces, God uses every piece and uses us in only a way that He can. Every broken piece can be put back together (restored) and be better used than before. When the pieces are put back together, that's when transformation begins. For every setback, I believe your faith becomes stronger. I encourage you to look back from whence you came and see where you are today—you are a testimony!

By now, many of you may be thinking if I wondered what the purpose of me having to go through these life challenges was, or wondering if I learned anything from them. There may not be a sound reason but what I do know is that Job lost all he had instantaneously, unlike myself, where it was more of periodic calamities. The Bible tells us that Job survived everything he went through, and in the end, he was blessed with more than what he ever had in terms of wealth. This gives me hope that I, too, can survive if it is the Lord's will. I accept that suffering is a part of life, and I am no different than other people. To survive, I need to remain steadfast in God's word. Accepting Jesus Christ as your personal Savior gives you the courage, endurance, strength and hope to keep striving, thriving and believing that through all of this, your testimony can be a catalyst or tool in helping someone to change their life, and then they too can spread the Good News that Jesus Saves.

Yes, it was and is a struggle to get back on my feet, but I continue to be determined and be resilient. The power of prayer is mighty. We are equipped with the power of prayer that changes things. Because Grace was on my right side and Mercy on my left, I will stand strong and with purpose and move forward and continue the battle towards victory. It is my prayer that God continue to elevate my mind and align my will with His will. I will continue trusting and believing in the Lord that soon my morning will come. I will remind myself to not get upset when my season is not what I think it should be. God knows best. "Be not weary in well doing." God can turn everything around for my good. And change can happen suddenly. But I must continue to trust in the Lord that it will be 'morning' again.

Epilogue

On my walk of faith, I learned not to get upset when my season was not what I thought it should be, knowing that God had rescued or delivered me before, and He will do it again. Be encouraged and know that there are no coincidences with God, though Satan would have you believe that your deliverance was coincidental, and use that as a method to turn you away from God. Though difficult to do, in your spiritual growth, use your darkness as a tool to grow, and do not concentrate on the negative. When thinking that God is taking too long to answer, just be patient. With me, my patience grew, especially with all the previous trials and tribulations I had experienced.

Romans 5:1-5: "Therefore being justified by faith, we have peace with God through our Lord Jesus Christ: By whom also we have access by faith into this grace wherein we stand, and rejoice in hope of the glory of God. And not only so, but we glory in tribulations also: knowing that tribulation worketh patience; And patience, experience; and experience, hope: And hope maketh not ashamed; because the love of God is shed

abroad in our hearts by the Holy Ghost which is given unto us."

During my waiting, I learned that God is continuing to build my trust and faith in Him, building up my tenacity and endurance level, similar to when Abraham was promised by God that his descendants would be delivered from slavery. God took them via the longer route, which was a way to build up their trust and faith in Him, their tenacity and their endurance levels.

When you are in the storm, you don't think about the times He bought you out, rather you're worrying about what's happening now. You are not remembering or focusing on the miracles He already performed or the doors He opened for you, or how He delivered you from previous surgeries or situations. When we are in the storm, we have the tendency to focus more on how to handle the situation or wonder how things are going to end, or rather praying those things work out in our favor. God knows best. He is working behind the scenes on our behalf. As I look back at what God has done for me, I cannot help but feel comforted in knowing that He loves me and has kept me this far.

This book was written in hopes to encourage, be aspirational and let you know that you are not alone in your journey. God allows us to be tested. Through your tests, your faith in God can prove that He is a miracle worker, and nothing is impossible. For those who are struggling with addiction, anguish or stress, it's fine to seek professional help, but also seek God. **Matthew 6:33** says, **"But seek ye first the kingdom of God, and his righteousness; and all these things shall be added unto you."** Know that you do not have to struggle alone. God is waiting on you to reach out to him. Again, I'm not saying that all of your struggles or troubles will be no longer, but what I can say is life will be different for the better if you accept Jesus Christ as your personal savior.

Keep moving to overcome challenges and live a victorious Christian life. Christ already won the victory; we just must walk in victory. God reminds us in his word that He will never leave us nor forsake us. **"Be strong and of a good courage, fear not, nor be afraid of them: for the LORD thy God, he it is that doth go with thee; he will not fail thee, nor forsake thee" (Deuteronomy 31:6).** Be encouraged. Keep the faith. May the favor of the Lord be with you.

Made in United States
North Haven, CT
25 April 2022

18546070R00102